Letters—May & James

A Private love
in a
Revolutionary
Year-

1916

Published by Bardic Press
71 Kenilworth Park
Harold's Cross
Dublin 6W
Ireland

ISBN:978-1-906834-29-6

Dedication

For my father, Joe Finn,
I began this project in honour of your 90th birthday and in memory
of the father you lost before you could know him
With love to Daddy

Contents

Preface

This is a delightful collection of letters that provides a window onto a past that is both familiar and distant to our own. It is an unselfconscious correspondence that allows us to glimpse snatched moments crystallised in time as the authors of the letters, James Finn and May Fay, worked through their blossoming love affair in the months during their engagement from January to June 1916.

There are several reoccurring themes beyond the personal. The topic of the letters themselves: writing them, waiting for them, and receiving them (even May's postman Paddie —often referred to as the 'bould Paddie' has a cameo role in the romance). Letters were the social media of their day, and May and James awaiting word from one another is no different from our waiting for the next text message or email.

James is clearly the more amorous, and possibly the more inse-cure of the two. There was 20 years age difference between them and James alternatively could not believe his good luck in May's agreeing to his proposal and his worrying that he was too old and not good enough for her. May's journey in their six months of courtship is the more visible, from her first letter in which she does not use the word 'love' actively (it takes her several months to do so as James courts her through words). In the first letter to him after the proposal she chooses her words carefully, writing to reassure him: 'I would not have consented to marry you if I did not like you very much.... I hope dear James that at some time I will be able to show you how much I appreciate your love' (14 January 1916), which, as the letters progress, and in their subsequent marriage, she clearly does.

There is much social history in this collection. One slowly comes to understand May's role as a key member of a farming household, and how her daily routine is punctuated by the dual rhythms of the farming lifecycle and the church calendar. James's responsibilities at work as an accountant in the National Health Commission would not be unfamiliar to those working in the public service today, even to the increase in working hours imposed by the British Government as a result of the war from 7 hours a day to 8 (4 April 1916).

There is, of course, the Great War which breaks through the very personal nature of the letters, and then, in April 1916, the Easter Rising. James is visiting May in Westmeath during Easter weekend, but upon his return to Dublin his letters provide news about the Rising and its aftermath interspersed with questions about the progress of the choosing and fitting of May's wedding dress, the ring he is purchasing for her, and news of the house renovations in Belgrave Square where May will join him as his new wife.

This is a precious collection of letters, made even more so by having both sides of the correspondence. These letters were a proxy for physical presence, and our lives are enriched by our being able to journey with these two lovely souls as they began their lives together, by the generosity of Tessa Finn in making them public, and who has so skilfully edited this edition, providing a wealth of background information that contextualises and enriches the collection.

Susan Schreibman
Professor of Digital Humanities,
Maynooth University

Introduction

Now that 2016 is upon us with the centenary of the Easter Rising in Ireland, there is a profusion of books about that time available in the bookshops, coming from a number of different angles; evaluating, re-thinking, celebrating the historical events of that year. Most will naturally focus on the figures that contributed to that eventful year; those who began the struggle, those who fought on the other side and those who became involved after the fighting had begun. This little book may serve as a side-dish to the feast; the people who are the focus here were going about their ordinary lives when the events broke out and though their sympathies were engaged they did not become actively involved in the struggle. But we do catch the references in their letters as they describe the things they witnessed and the rumours they heard and it helps you to see how many of the other ordinary people of Dublin at the time would have experienced it too.

The letters

These letters are part of my family's inheritance, lovingly treasured by my grandmother, May Fay Finn. She had every reason to cling on to these reminders of the love of her life, my grandfather James Finn. They were married not quite six years when he died leaving her, twenty-five years old and seven months pregnant with their fourth child. She never seems to have considered remarriage, yet she was lovely to the end.

She was nineteen when she got engaged, twenty when she

married him, though it would seem she had known him for
years. She lived in Westmeath on a farm on the slopes of the Hill

of Uisneach. He was nearly twenty years older than her, living in
Dublin but often came to stay at the home of her near neighbour,
Mrs. Mary Seery, widow of his cousin Tom. He says in the letters
that he had long had his eye on her but was embarrassed by the
age difference then evidently at Christmastime 1915 he must
have plucked up his courage and she said yes and so our series of
letters begin.

This book is written to commemorate them and their love. It
also gives an insight into the world of rather ordinary people in an
historical year. As May says they were "not very rebellious char-
acters"; James was progressing well in a promising career in the
Empire's Civil Service - they feared conscription, resented high-
handed administration but were accustomed to the idea of Ireland's role as part of the Union, seeing a solution in Home Rule.

From the comments in the letters you can see how their loyalty becomes swayed and turned under the violence of Easter week and the following period. Like many others they endured the anguish of being separated from each other and other loved ones during those chaotic weeks, the circulating rumours, emerging truths. And then life returns to some normality and the wedding preparations continue.

At the beginning May is really just a girl; her handwriting Is open and loopy, her spelling charmingly chaotic- I've made it a bit easier to understand in my transcriptions – but it's fun to see how her handwriting "grows up" in the period of these letters.
After the wedding they move into 39 Belgrave Square with James' mother Bridget and sisters Nora and Moll- not every girl's dream, but May was up to it! Bridget, Nora and Moll later moved into a house on Dunville Avenue, a short distance away.
In the following years first Seamus (James Pearse, 1917), then Enna (Eithne, 1918) and Ita (1920) were born. Sometime in 1917 James had contracted the flu in the great Flu epidemic. He survived but, as was quite common, the endocarditis it caused left him with heart damage to which he succumbed in 1922 when May was pregnant with their fourth child, Joseph. It seems he had time enough to say goodbye and write a will. His last act was to write May a check for the remains of his bank account, in case she might have difficulty accessing it (which in the event she did not). The grief of their final parting is hard to imagine, but May was a survivor and succeeded against the odds to attract adequate means and bring up her children and she had great joy in her grandchildren.

There are a lot of references in the letters, to relatives, neighbours' gossip and to current affairs. I've tried my best to investigate and place those references and explain them in endnotes. Some things I was not able to clear up, so they remain a mystery. To me, the attraction in this collection is the intimate insight it gives, so I have not edited out the minutiae, I hope you will enjoy this window into a world.

James Edward Finn

James Edward Finn was born May 26th 1876, only son of James Joseph Finn and Bridget Gavagan Finn. His father, who had been a member of the Revenue Police, died aged 48 in 1883 when James was still only six years old. Bridget then worked as a Postmistress in Dysart, County Westmeath (near her family home).

The widow's only son had to work hard and he was bright, it is said that James won a scholarship, presumably to a boarding school, possibly St Vincent's College, Castleknock (they seem to have a record of him there at least between 1891 and 1893. The Finns had close ties to their Finn cousins, Mary, James Patrick ("Jim") and Jane ("Baby"). When their uncle Lawrence Finn had died in 1888, his wife abandoned the children and they were brought up in care of their relatives.

The 1911 wedding of James' cousin Mary Finn Hanley. Left to right: Top; Canon J Glynn, Bridget Finn, Jim Finn. Bottom; Jane "Baby" Finn, James Finn, Mary and Hugh Hanley

On July 30th 1895 (age 19) he was accepted into the civil service after open competition as a clerk second division. It's unclear but I think it was in London where he started his career. In 1898 he appears in that role working in GPO Dublin in the accountants' department (his immediate superior was D.P. Gallagher).

While James is still in training, his sister Margaret is supporting the family as postmistress in Castletown Geoghegan. In the 1901 census we find her aged 22 with sisters Nora and Moll working under her. James doesn't appear in the census, he was presumably living in Dublin but maybe he was travelling at the time. In one of the family mysteries Margaret disappears from the family story soon after. She died in 1909 of septopyaemia in Cork Street Fever Hospital, Dublin and was never mentioned again.

Sandymount village Dublin

In Dublin, between 1905 and 1908, James initially lived in Sandymount but by the time of the 1911 census he has come up in the world and is living in what must be larger accommodation in Charlestown Avenue, Rathmines with his mother, sister Moll and cousin Jim (Nora was working in Drogheda at the time), by 1912 he has moved in to 39 Belgrave Square, where he was still living in 1916. On March 29th 1912 he was transferred to the new National Health Insurance Commission(Ireland) in their grand offices in Pembroke House on Mount Street, the former home of the Lord Chancellor Samuel Walker- there were different commisions set up in Great Britain and Ireland after David Lloyd George's National Health Insurance Bill of 1911- and later promoted to assistant accountant under the same D.P. Gallagher who is mentioned often in the letters, mostly rather indulgently, just as "The Accountant".

The Irish Times - Saturday, March 16, 1912

NEW PREMISES FOR IRISH INSURANCE COMMISSIONERS.

The address of the National Health Insurance Commissioners for Ireland, as from the 13th inst., will be Pembroke House, Upper Mount street, Dublin. This fine building was formerly the residence of the late Lord Chancellor, the Right Hon. Sir Samuel Walker, and is in every respect commodious and central. It is not, however, intended to retain it as the permanent headquarters of the Irish Commissioners, since a more suitable building will in due course be provided by the Board of Works; but, in the meantime, it should answer its purpose particularly well. Readers should note that inquiries intended for the Commissioners should be addressed to Pembroke House, and not to Dawson Chambers, the former offices of the Commission.

MARY "MAY" FAY

May Fay was born May 17th 1896, daughter of Edward Fay and Annie Dardis Fay. She was the fourth in a family of eight, living on a good farm on the slopes of Uisneach in Westmeath. Like James, she also lost her father when she was six years old. Edward Fay died in 1902 aged 45 before his youngest son Ned was born.

From June 1901 the farm must have been very crowded, for her maternal aunt Minnie Wynne, uncle Edward and six cousins moved in, having been evicted from Mearescourt Estate because of Edward Wynne's activity in the Land War. When a meeting to protest against the Mearscourt evictions was prohibited the locals held four meetings at different locations, all this gained widespread coverage. Sometime in 1909 the Wynne family were reinstated to their land at Mearescourt, though Edward had died in the meantime.

In early 1901 they received word from Argentina that May's paternal uncle Tim and aunt Ellen had died, leaving their 8 children orphaned. May's mother received a letter asking her if she could take them in, but regretfully felt she could not. For many years

The family farm in Togherstown

that was the last contact but in recent years the family have re-connected with the emigrants. May went to school in St Joseph's Convent Boarding School in Ferbane County Offaly to which she refers in her letters.There are also references to her sister Jenny's marriage in 1915 to John "Jack" Corbett in Mitchelstown, in 1916 a job was found there for her brother Tim, this was later to have consequences for him since he got involved in the Civil War there, but that is outside the remit of this book..

May Fay's parents, Edward and Annie Dardis Fay

The three Fay sisters; Jenny, May and Nano against a backdrop
of the farm in Togherstown

The Letters

39, Belgrave Square,
Rathmines,
Dublin.

13th January 1906

My dearest May,

I got back safe and sound although I don't feel quite so cheerful as I did in the country. I always feel like that but I had more reason, I suppose, this time than ever before.

I remember now that on Monday when I spoke to you I was so intent on asking you to

39 Belgrave Square
Rathmines
Dublin
13ᵗʰ January 1916

My Dearest May

I got back safe and sound although I didn't feel quite so cheerful as I did in the country. I always feel like that but I had more reason, I suppose, this time than ever before.

I remember now that on Monday when I spoke to you I was so intent on asking you to marry me that I quite overlooked in the excitement telling you that I loved you very dearly. I hope you didn't need me to tell you that anyhow in order to believe it of me. I can hardly yet think that the converse is true, that you have any special regards for me – it seems somehow too good to be true but I hope with God's help that it may come true anyhow. As I told you already I could never bring myself to believe that any good girl could trust herself to me and in your case it seemed impossible but I suppose the reason is that the Lord is always a thousand times better to us than we deserve. With his help I will try to be better in the future than I have been in the past and maybe in the end with you to help me I'll turn out something better than the rotter I know myself to be.

This is a queer sort of a letter to write to you, you will think, but perhaps you will be able to read between the lines that I love you whatever comes and that if the Lord spares me I will try and do my duty to you.

Mrs Seery¹ showed you my mother's letter, I presume. You will see that she is as pleased as can be with events. Indeed I think she has always wished that I might be lucky enough to get you. Now that the 100 to 1 chance has come off, we are both naturally delighted.

No news here since I went away. Am back in harness tomorrow but will take a few days off when you come up which I hope will be soon. Give my regards to everyone and with dearest love to yourself,

Yours forever,
James

Togherstown,
Ballinea,
Mullingar.
14-1-1916.

My dearest James,

I was delighted
to get your letter this morn
you were very good to
write so soon I was not
expecting it tho' I was

Togherstown
Ballinea
Mullingar
14/1/1916

My Dearest James,

I was delighted to get your letter this morn you were very good to write so soon I was not expecting it tho' I was hoping you would I am quite looking forward to seeing you the week after next, I did feel a wee bit lonely after you leaving and you may be quite sure I would not have consented to marry you if I did not like you very much & that for some time but I never thought I would be so fortunate as to get a warm corner in your heart, I hope dear James that at some time I will be able to show you how much I appreciate your love.

Mother has decided on going to see Jennie[2] Monday next- had a letter from her yesterday saying she was not feeling so well & would like to see her she expects to be back about Monday I hope she will anyway so that I can get up to see you, if Mrs S is ready then.

Your Mother wrote me a very nice letter I am delighted she is so pleased with me, I'm sure we will be very happy together I will write to her tomorrow.

[scribbled on side in pencil] This was late for the post last night I think you will have it tonight (Sat) I have just opened it here the PO Mullingar to tell you the reason of the delay

Love from May,
Bye Bye now dearest James

39 Belgrave Square
Rathmines
Dublin
16/1/1916

My dear, dear Girl,

This will have to be a short letter if I am to catch the post so I hope you will forgive me. I need hardly tell you how delighted I was to have your dear letter and to see by it that you have a real affection for me. I know that I don't deserve it and I keep wondering all the time what I have ever done to deserve such a blessing. I suppose good intentions sometimes earn a reward such as your love is and I know anyway that my present intentions are sincere and good. I hope, however badly the execution may turn out, with you to help me perhaps it may not be so bad as I sometimes fear.

Well, my dearest, I was sorry to see you won't be able to come up as soon as I had hoped but I must only have patience till I see you. I'm sorry to hear that Jennie is knocked up but of course it is nothing serious. It's a good thing your mother has decided to go down and see her for I'm sure she wouldn't be contented till she saw her mother. They will have a lot to say to each other so perhaps she may not come back as soon as I hope. However there's no use in my being selfish anyhow; I ought to be more than thankful with things as they are and I am too.

Tell Christy and Tommy Seery[3] that a friend of mine heard English cattle buyers at Dublin market on Thursday saying that beef will be 1/6 a lb. on the beast's back before a month. So they had better stiffen their prices for any stall feds they have remaining. From all I hear everything points to very high prices for cattle in the near future. So they'd better avail of the tip.

My mother was delighted to have such a very nice letter from Mrs Fay this morning. She let me see it and I must say I was honestly amused with her good opinion of this miserable sinner. I can hardly help laughing every time I hear people gassing about my goodness. Hope this catches the post so must shut up with my heart's warmest love to the best little girl in the world. Please don't laugh. It's true.

Yours ever fondly, James

My dearest James,
     Your nice letter was indeed very welcome this morn I was watching out for it but I had long given up when Paddie[4] arrived about 12:30 we were expecting a line from Mother but did not get one still I suppose she is safe or we would hear before this.
I had a very nice letter from Moll[5] although I have never had the pleasure of meeting her. It was very good of her to write. M. Joe Wynne[6] wrote me saying how delighted she was about my engagement & what a lucky girl I was, for myself I cannot imagine even yet one like you could be content with a plain country girl of course the thought that you are really fond of me makes me very, very happy but I cannot help letting my worthlessness in every way rest very heavily on my mind.
About going to town I see now it was all for the best we allowed Mother off first; had we decided on taking the longed for visit on Sat I certainly would be left.
The cold I had the day you left which seemed nothing proved much worse than I even knew it did until last night I was very restless coughing & smothering etc. I remained in bed until very late today but Thank God I feel quiet (sic) on the mend now
I am managing to keep the "blossoms" off my lips & nose by means of Corbett[7]'s ointment so I expect I will feel really fit by the time Mother comes home.
Tommy Seery spent last night with us, his mother being in Ballymore, he said it was a "God's charity" I had no one to do anything for my cold- what made I leave my own road & he always so nice to me. Mrs S. says everyone in there is delighted with the news. Josephine[8] wrote me good wishes thro' Mrs Seery would have sent wires to us both but was afraid of being laughed at. Mrs S says she is very jealous at not hearing from you but sends warmest love I was in town (Mullingar) Sat last I paid a long promised visit to Brother Leary I was very glad to get out of him notwithstanding how nice he was to me took me on his knee put his arm around my neck in fact did everything but kissed me. I was going to tell him I'd tell you but thought it better not.

What you said of me in the end of your letter did indeed make me laugh and laugh hearty, I was going to tell Nano what I was laughing at but I knew drinking would be her first thought.

Bye Bye now dearest James

Lots of love from your own May

REMARKABLE EVIDENCE OF AN R.I.C. MAN.

R.I.C., Boston, Tubber, Co. Clare,

Mr. J. Corbett, M.P.S.I.,
Mitchelstown

Dear Sir—I am sending for some more Corn Cure; what you sent me proved invaluable, but half of it was used up by other fellows. I am surprised if you have not got applications by now for more of it. However, I circulated it as widely as possible, but none more than it deserved.

Send me on more by return, please, as I have the devil nearly taken out.—I remain, your faithfully,

JOHN MURRAY.

This is only one specimen of the many testimonials received for this wonderful Corn Remedy. Is sold in packets at 10d., post free, and is guaranteed to cure.

Address—J. CORBETT, M.P.S.I.,
Mitchelstown, Co. Cork.
—(Advt.)

Jenny Fay's husband Jack Corbett was a pharmacist who sold a number of house recipe remedies

National Health Commission (Ireland)
Pembroke House
Upper Mount Street
Dublin
21/1/1916

My darling May

I have a minute or two to spare so I had better drop you a line. I got your letter yesterday but could not manage to find time yesterday to reply and shall have very little time now either so you must let me down light if I can't write much. I was very sorry indeed to hear of the cold and that it was so very near having the lamentable results of producing blossoms on your nose and lips.

What on earth would I do if that happened and I looking forward so anxiously to see you and – with pluck- to kiss you in a few days. However all's well that ends well and I will pray for Corbett until my dying day if his ointment cures the complaint in time.

I was very jealous to hear about Brother Leary's conduct. I begin to see that if a man has only cheek enough he can do anything so you'd better look out for trouble when I see you. By the way while I think of it, I don't see why you only received my letter on the 19th. I wrote to you on Sunday the 16th in time for post so you should have had my letter by Monday or Tuesday at the very latest. I expect the *bould* Paddie is neglecting his duties.

Mrs Seery's message is a rebuke to me for not writing. If I can manage a moment at all I will write to her today but tell her in any case I bear her in mind even tho' I didn't write. I'll have to keep her on my hands for another few months anyhow. I was glad to hear of Josephine and M .Joe Wynne congratulations. I accept them for myself anyhow- in your case I'm not so sure but it should be sympathy that should be offered you. That reminds me that it's rather a shame for you to be "pulling my leg" about the plain country girl and her worthlessness. Don't you know very well you're about a million times too good for a chap like me? As I hope for mercy, I can tell you that I have asked God's pardon every day since you promised me for having cheated you into marriage with me. As I'm writing this in the office you won't I suppose suspect me of not being quite sober so I can say again that I love you, May, and will, I hope, till the end.

Always your loving, James

[Postcard dated 22/1?]
Mullingar

James Dearest,

I was very glad to get your letter this morn it cheered me as I was feeling lonely not feeling so well & then Mother being away fancy she never wrote to us since she left but asked in a letter to Mrs. S. did we get her card she is staying till Monday but when that day comes she'll will stay until another I hope when she does come I will feel fit to start on that so much wished for visit Hope you will excuse this short note in answer to your nice letter

Your ever loving May

I met Mrs Priest (?) Moran[9] today she wanted to know from Mrs. S- was I the one was engaged to her friend? It was a start to see it had travelled so far

Good news
you know

Sackville Street Dublin

39 Belgrave Square
Rathmines
Dublin
23/1/1916

My dearest May,

I came down to breakfast this morning with a wild hope that I might have a note from you but without any real expectation of it because I knew Saturday would be a busy day with you in addition to your being the sole housekeeper at present. Needless to say therefore how overjoyed I was to get your dear note. Even although it was a short one, I'd rather have it than the finest literature in the English language. I was very sorry indeed to see that you are not yet quite well and I sincerely trust- selfishness as usual- that it won't interfere with my seeing you this week. It is sweet of you to say that you are looking forward to your visit to Dublin.

You can imagine how I look forward to it and to seeing my dear girl in a few days more. Please don't get into the dumps again. If you do, I'll be tempted to think you're getting sorry for your bargain. Just to cheer you up I'll tell you a joke. I was coming home one day about a week ago and as usual I was thinking about you- I may confess that this is a habit of about three years standing- I looked up suddenly and there was <u>Venus</u> shining down on me benevolently from the evening sky. This is gospel truth- and ever since I have her company on the way home in the evening. If you like to see for yourself, you'll see her any evening about half an hour after sunset in the western sky. You can't mistake her as you can't see any other stars so early after sunset. So now you know. I wrote to Mrs Seery as well as yourself. So I hope that will remove her jealousy and keep her in good humour till I can see you both. I was waylaid on O'Connell Bridge yesterday by Josephine, Mrs George and Kathleen[10] and had to stand the usual chaff from them all. Mrs G said I was a sly boy. Now I wonder and I thought that everyone could see as plain as possible that I was after you for a very long time past. To tell truth the only thing I ever found wrong with you was your age. I was always ashamed to speak and so I put it off although I have the idea at the back of my head for the last three or four years.

Well, my dearest dear, it's twelve midnight now so I must close
up. I couldn't manage to write in time for post and know I
shouldn't have time tomorrow but you'll have this on Tuesday.
Let me know early what day you're coming. I shall close here with
warmest love and kisses to my dearest girl.
Goodbye, dear
Your loving James

Togherstown
24/1

My darling little man,
I just see this chance of posting a line to you hope
you got card from Mullingar Mother wrote saying she is coming
home tomorrow (Tues) so we are off on Sat next If I am not the
obstical (sic) again. I would not be at all surprised If I was getting
the mumps. I feel my neck very sore of course they are not very
dangerous but Mother would never let me on that journey with
them God send tho' it is nothing at all No more time so goodbye
with all my best love
Yours May

25/1

My dearest James,
Your letter this morn was indeed a very pleasant surprise I
was not expecting a line from you so soon, Yesterday I wrote you
a note saying I had mumps. I was frightened hearing everyone
say they are so dangerous for grownup people they are nothing at all at least they won't prevent my going to town on Sat if
Mother is home by that time, Jennie sent us a letter today saying
she is keeping her until Thursday, that is alright if she does not
keep her longer you know I am anxious for her return for the one
reason still I encourage her to stay for Jennie's sake- she is so far
from home & Mother's visits will I think be few & far between so
you will understand if we don't get off as soon as we expected
but I am sure we won't be later than Monday. It is not so long to
wait tho' it seems like a month since Mother left.
You say you have been thinking of me for so long that
no doubt makes me feel Oh! so flattered & happy still it is hardly
possible for me to believe it since it is scarcely a year since you

came to know me at all, that is when I was up this time last year.
A few months before that about but I suppose you do not remember we met on a train you did not know me and, as well as I
can remember, we did not speak - my fault I suppose. I was with
Jennie & Jack. So now- I must watch out for Venus perhaps this
evening

Mrs Seery has just been here now with a letter to your Mother for
the post telling her we will go on Sat so that looks good for us.
Jerome[11] was down on Sun. In the even Messers Johnnie & Ned[12]
went to Balrath[13] , the boys I heard lost heavily at the cards in a
short time.

Mrs S heard the Kilbeggan bride diet? read to a very low degree
she was very angry with the Dancers for putting in their horse
there disturbing her father etc[14] . I know you won't feel hurt at
the lack of friendship there if you did I would not tell you. Jack
Nolan[15] is out there working today- he was to dinner & when all
were gone he said "curse you'd be thinking yourself too good for
a decent farmer as well as the rest" I said I was afraid I would- he
shook his head & went out- he must have been making a match
for me he, often tried that on with Jennie you know.

I fancy you have enough of this so I will say good bye with warmest love but keeping the kisses for a long time yet, thanks, for you
tho'.

your ever loving May

Togherstown
Ballinea
26/1/16

My dearest James
        Your letter was very welcome this morn. The
mumps are just the same but may be improved by Sat they
did not swell up with me like they did with the boys I don't feel
knocked out in any way except I can't eat solid food.

About going up on Friday I'm very sorry to say we could not possible get off Mother will be home late Thursday & Friday all the
boys are going to the fair in Moate then if we can at all manage to
get a driver we will leave by the early train it is only a chance tho'
but there is no doubt about the midday train Sat even if I have
two big lumps each side of my face How would you like to see

me like that? You should feel very much inclined to throw up your claim I think, however I'll chance it.
No news today so Good bye till Sat. Roll on long days-
   Your ever loving May

                                                                    27/1
   My darling girl,
      This is going to be a very short note indeed. Glad to see from your letter today that mumps are better and that we may really hope to see you both on Saturday! If you are coming by first train <u>let me know </u>as I should like to meet you at the station. Shall be on tenterhooks until then. By the way wasn't a bit hurt over Miss Gertie Kelly's remarks about the dancers. I suppose you'll see the marriage in Dublin next week[16] if you care to turn up at the church. Where is it to be and is Father McNamara going to pull the bolt. If they're looking for a cheap job they should go to the registry office as John[17] threatened he would. Remember me to your mother and Mrs S.
   your loving little man
   James

                                                       Togherstown
                                                          Ballinea
                                                          27/1/16

   My dearest James
      Was delighted to get your letter this morn. You are very good to think of writing so often.
Mother is coming today she had written to say so but sent a wire also it took a start out of us thought she was lost for something wrong, is the first thing the sight of a wire puts into our heads
Well for <u>sure</u> & for <u>certain</u> we are going on Sat midday train from Castletown you may tell your (our) Mother so & also tell her Mrs S-will not write to her when I'm writing & not to be depending on her for butter that she has not<u> enough for herself</u>.
I am very glad we are getting off on Sat late train & all we could not manage first. The mumps are improved today I expect by tomorrow or Sat at least I'll be able to eat something
Mrs S- is afraid today she is getting them she might get them from mere fear I hope she won't anyway they are nasty without being dangerous of course Laddie, Tim[18] & Edgar[19] have had them & colds before that so everything happened while Mother

was away.

Jack Nolan knows nothing but I think he can be justly suspected of having just an outline of people's minds. Poor Jack he is thinking of listing not to save his king & country but to save his wife & family from starving I expect. He is getting a bit anxious about Jonnie[20] 's long holiday, nothing much escapes him he has near given up hopes of anyone thinking of me seems to think I ought to be gone by that. I must be grown up & for some time too. I will not write any more now so keep this love warm till Sat

Your ever loving

May

On Saturday 29th January, May came up to Dublin accompanied by her mother to visit her betrothed and his family in Rathmines, a vibrantly growing suburb town of Dublin with an expanding population of the new catholic middle class such as James Finn. James had rented number 39 Belgrave Square since 1912. With him lived his mother and sisters Nora and Mary "Moll". Shortly thereafter May's little brother Tim (15) is to travel to Mitchelstown where he has the opportunity of a job, presumably organized by Jack Corbett, Jenny's husband.

Belgrave Square Rathmines

James' sister Nora, standing and mother, Bridget Gavagan Finn seated

Togherstown
Ballinea
8th Feb 1916

My dearest James

We got home safely last night the drive from the station was cold & dreary I suppose I felt it all the more not being in the best of spirits, the ground is covered with snow today so the fire is my best friend

I found all well. Tim will leave for Mitchelstown next week Jennie thinks she'll never get him down. We will be lonely for him some-one will have to go as far as Portarlington²¹ with him I think. Mother and all liked my ring they thought we'd have the time fixed but that is easier said than done for <u>important people like us.</u>

I must come at mother anyway to settle the time, we must at least fix it up when you come down next time we won't have long to look forward to that visit I hope. Were you lonely Monday night for someone to sit up with you? I was thinking of you when I was going to bed about eleven o'clock and I felt very down in the boots but no one is ever any the wiser of my feeling I might feel better if there were someone. You will have to excuse this letter I don't know how you can read writing etc

Can I hope to have a letter in the morn but you may be too busy Give my love to your Mother & & Nora I must write to your mother I am sure she is glad to get shut of us.

Tons of warmest love from
May

National Health Commission (Ireland)
Pembroke House
Upper Mount Street
Dublin
9th Feby 1916

My dearest girl

This is going to be a divil of a scribble if I'm going to catch the post. I was overwhelmed with work yesterday and couldn't get a moment to write so that if you are looking out for a letter today I'm afraid you will be disappointed. Well my dearest, I was glad to have your letter this morning and to see by it (selfish beast) that you were a bit lonely at leaving Dublin. For myself I must say I felt rotten on Monday night with the result that I went to bed before eleven in order to escape from my loneliness. Today I feel a bit more cheerful but I need hardly say I shall be looking forward anxiously to a visit to the country in the next few weeks. I must say that you are a silly girl to be worrying your head over me or whether I was lonely (not lovely) or not. However I hope there is a good time coming when we can sit round the fire at night and nobody to say boo to us.

As regards fixing the day I have been worrying over it since a good deal. My only objection to May (the month not the girl) is that it's a bad time for holidays and as we shall never have a holiday again quite like the one, I'd like for your sake to have good weather. However I suppose we can leave further discussion of this over until I see you when we can settle the matter one way or another without trouble. Glad to hear everyone liked your ring. I'm sure poor Jenny will be anxious to have Tim down. I can sympathise with her in that anyhow but I expect he'll be a bit lonely for a while. It's a good job for him to get a start so nicely.

I think everyone at home was a bit lonesome for the visitors as well as myself. My mother didn't seem to be quite herself since. Moll is coming home this evening for a few days preparatory to going out to Kingstown to her new job. I haven't seen her yet but I expect she will be quite out of her skin with joy over the prospect of a change from Newbridge. Don't know when I can get down to see you. Don't care to go unless I can get a day or two off but you may expect me anyhow not later than Saturday fortnight (26th Feby). Hope you'll give me a kiss when I go my way. Give my regards to your mother and all and also Mrs Seery. Words fail to say what love I send yourself.

Your ever loving and devoted
James

Togherstown
Ballinea
Mullingar
Undated

My dearest James

I was glad to get your letter this morn the post was late & I was just beginning to feel very cross when Mrs Post[22] put her beautiful face round the door- there was a letter also from Mary Kelly[23] Castletown you know the only remark she made about us was "I heard of May's choice" not a wish or another word.

The bride & groom are coming home next week. Jimmy Duffy, Rose Kelly's man, is spending his holidays in Balrath at present, himself and Dan having a royal time. J. Cunningham heard nothing yet Josephine[24] called here yesterday to congratulate me she was in great humour I must surely write to your Mother tomorrow I'm such a bad hand at the pen that I hate taking it up but it is so ungrateful not to have written straight away. Mother is in Mullingar today, we are a bit busy- I am giving this letter to the breadman to post. I hope it will go alright All hands think I got fat while I was away. The change did me a lot of good anyway. I can't say I would like to get anything fatter tho' I got through most of performances in the Abbey they enjoyed them if you ever come across that Dialogue "The Work House Ward[25]" give it to me I'd like to show it to the lads.

No news at all except lots of warmest love from your only dot-ing little girl

EMPIRE THEATRE
6 40 .... TWICE NIG-.LY 90
L A S T   W E E K
BARNEY ARMSTRONG'S
RECORD SUCCESS,
CINDERELLA
LAST MATINEE, SATURDAY, 5th

TIVOLI 7 OC. 9 OC. TIVOLI
      Tel. 4125
6 MUSICAL WILL LACEY,
LONGSHOREMEN.   Cycling Comedian.
The Deldes, Gordon and Beal, May Locke.
Spear and Lacce, Harry Balcoo, Pathe Gazette.
PREMIER QUARTETTE——Lady Vocalists.
A24319

THE ABBEY THEATRE.
THIS (THURSDAY) and Following Evenings at
8.15 p.m., and SATURDAY MATINEE, at 2.30 p m.
THE BRIBE,
A Play in Three Acts, by SEUMAS O KELLY.
THE WORKHOUSE WARD,
A Comedy in One Act, by LADY GREGORY.
Prices.—3s, 2s, 1s 6d, 1s. and 6d No 6d
Seats at Matinee. Booking at Theatre Tel.
5005.   A24206

ROTUNDA DAILY AT 3 P.M.
TWICE NIGHTLY, at   PICTURES
8.45 AND 9
EXPLOITS OF ELAINE (16).
THE CRYPTIC RING,
Sensational Drama (in Two Acts)
' FATAL RESEMBLANCE '
Powerful Dramatic story (in Two Parts)
A24381

THE PICTURE HOUSE,
GRAFTON STREET, DUBLIN.
MISS MARIE TEMPEST in a delightful Four-part
Comedy,
MRS PLUM'S PUDDING
Also ' The Revenge of the Steeplejack (Drama).
Sir James Mortimer s Wager (Comic).

National Health Commission (Ireland)
Pembroke House
Upper Mount Street
Dublin
11th Feb 1916

My darling May

Your letter received this morning as expected. Fortunately I have no need to watch out for the beautiful figure of Mrs Lonican[26] who I have no doubt is praying for me for all the extra work I am putting on herself and her good man. However let's hope that the extra work won't be for too long and that one of these fine days we'll be in the position of not needing to write letters to each other, unless it is across the breakfast table. I was interested to hear of Mrs Kelly's good wishes. She may not be so bad as she seems all the same. I think I told you about Jim[27] - he never said anything either when I told him and yet I know very well he wished me all good luck. Some people are like that and maybe she's one of them.

Saw a note from Mrs Seery this morning. It seems that Mrs Kiernan[28] wrote to her the day before with the news of John Duffy's marriage but the letter didn't reach. I hope we won't have such a queer marriage when we go off the hooks. Glad to hear everybody thought you so much improved by your stay in the town and hope you will do as well when you come permanently. Perhaps the present improvement is due to the fact that you were so lazy in the mornings and that it will pass off now that you have to earn your crust again.

Talking of crusts, I'm earning mine these days. We have just had what they call a Departmental committee appointed to consider the simplification of the Insurance act. The most of the inquiries turn on questions of accounting on which I am the Irish expert. Result is that your darling little man is nearly killed. However I have weathered worse storms than the present one and hope to keep my end up all right and to do credit to the Irish Commission. Glad to hear you have been giving theatrical recitals to the boys and that they enjoyed them. I'm going to the Abbey tonight with my mother & Moll and will be thinking of you. Wish you were with me but will see you any how in a fortnight. Tell Mrs Seery to keep the bed warm till then (Johnnie I suppose will do so anyhow). I will enquire about J. one of these days if he doesn't hear but he had better let me know whether he would be willing to come up or not. Remember me to all at home and in Lockard-stown[29] . I send you my dearest love and every warm wish of my heart..

Ever your loving James

Togherstown
Ballinea
Mullingar
12th Feb 1916

My own dearest James
        I got your letter today I was sorry to know they are work-ing you so hard. I would like to write to the authorities on your behalf only I'm not really too well acquainted there. In earnest I hope you won't have to continue hard work for me this is a very lazy time sleeping and eating is our chief work the most I did since I came home was a bit of sewing for Tim -with my hand, the machine being out of order.
First to amuse you I must tell you I answered Mary Kelly's let-ter, gave our order[30] , told her I called on Aggie & Jennie & said I was very jealous she never wrote to wish me joy, she wrote back (order etc thanks) Glad you called on A.& J[31] - How is Laddie[32] ?
I am dearest May your fond cousin Mary. Isn't that very good? We don't heed at all. The Bride & Groom were due in Castletown Monday. I think Dan Kiernan gives them one week together- says he heard it in Castetown. I wonder how long they will give us.
I hope you enjoyed the Abbey with your Mother & Moll What was on? Indeed I wish I were with you I will be very lonely tomorrow I wish I had ~~told~~ asked you to send me a line that I would have to rise my heart don't think by that I am really down hearted- I am not-all the same I am wishing to see you. I suppose you will not get more till the week end. Jonnie has not heard anything yet-I am always ashamed to look on my letters- I write so badly but I know at least I hope they are nonetheless welcome for that.
        My dearest James I will say goodbye with all my love & several xxxxxxx
        From your loving
        May

39 Belgrave Square
Rathmines
Dublin
13th Feb 1916

My dearest May

I was delighted as usual to find your dear letter waiting
for me this morning and indeed when I did at last get up I was as
much ashamed of having made it wait as if it was yourself that
had been waiting for me. I was more than usually pleased with
the contents for I am vain enough to think from reading it that
you do think of me and that you are anxious to see me again.
Well, my dearest dear, it won't be very long now. I'll surely make
a burst to see you on Saturday week and it will go very bad with
me if I'm not able to spin out the visit to Tuesday or Wednesday
after; so now be a good little divil and say your prayers and you'll
see the treat that God will send you. What you say about asking
me to write to you for Sunday to "rise your heart" makes me awfully vain- really and truly it does- so if you don't want me to get a
swelled head you had better not be buttering me up in that way.
I really will begin to fancy myself soon if you tell me stories like
that. All the same it does me good to know that you have such a
regard and opinion of me and I feel sure it helps me in trying to
be worthy of you. Anyhow in future I promise that you will have
a letter from me every Sunday without fail. I was amused to hear
about Mrs Kelly. It's just what I'd do myself to put it up to her to
wish me joy for the pleasure of putting her in a hole.
I hope for everybody's sake that John Duffy and the Mrs will last
longer than Dan Kiernan says. I saw Dan at the Broadstone the
evening you were going home. I don't know whether he was late
for the train or what but it was after it left he came waddling up
the platform. I enjoyed the Abbey very much the other night.
There were two short comedies one "The Coiner" and "The Or-
angemen" and a play by Geo. Bernard Shaw "The Shewing-Up of
Blanco Posnet". The Shaw play was easily the best but I'm afraid
it would shock you here and there. The conversation at times was
a bit open but I finished up nearly in tears so admit I'm a sentimental donkey (?)

THE BAND OF THE R.D.F

Prices:—Boxes, £2 2s., £1 10s., £1 1s.; Dress Circle, 5s.; Balcony, 4s.; Parterre, 3s.; Upper Circle, 2s. (tickets purchased before the 4th guarantee a seat); Gallery, 1s. (tickets purchased before the 4th admit by Early Door).

THE COLISEUM THEATRE.
TO-NIGHT, JACK
8.45 and 9.0. AND JILL.
LAST PERFORMANCES.
MATINEE TO-DAY AT 2.30,
WHEN CHILDREN 1/-, 6d., 3d., and 2d.
BOX OFFICE 10 a.m. to 10 p.m. 'PHONE 2020.
NEXT WEEK, "FORTY
ENTIRE CHANGE. THIEVES."

THE ABBEY THEATRE.
MATINEE THIS (SATURDAY) AFTERNOON AT 2.30, and THIS EVENING AT 8.15 p.m.
A NEW PLAY, by Bernard Duffy, entitled
The Coiner,
The Shewing-up of Blanco Posnet,
By Bernard Shaw.
The Orangeman,
By St. John Ervine.

PRICES:—3/-, 2/-, 1/6, 1/-, and 6d. No. 6d. Seats at Matinee. Booking at Theatre. Tel. 3268.
Last Saturday several hundred playgoers were turned away from the Abbey Theatre because the house was full. The same thing happened on the previous Saturday. If you wish to be sure of a seat this Saturday book it now. 2026

FEIS CEOIL, 1916.
MAY 8th to 13th.

Irish Independent Feb 12 1916

There are two very good plays on next week also which I wish you could see. You'd enjoy both of them I feel sure, Tell Mrs Seery that I'll inquire about Johnnie[34] and let her know and that I'll watch for any chance I see anywhere. Don't worry about the work. I always enjoy it and I'm old enough to fight my own corner. Give my love to all. What can I say to yourself, dearest, but that I _love_ you with every loving wish and thought.
    Yours devotedly
    James

[added later]
Thanks for the kisses. I'm afraid you wouldn't be so generous if they were other than paper kisses. However I hope for the best and look forward impatiently to my reward _perhaps_ when I see you again. What do you say?
    James

Togherstown
Ballinea
14th Feb 1916

My own dearest James,
    Your letter this morn was indeed a pleasant surprise I thought a letter posted Sunday in the City would not land here till Tuesday my letter written home Sunday before I left was not as soon as myself.

I am very glad you have decided on coming it will be well to get Tues or Wed I did not think you would I must make Mother settle the time for us. There is nothing doing here today. Tim is going or gone & Mother is very lonely. I knew she would be. Tim was lonely in the end his schoolfellows (two) were very sorry for him. In fact everyone that knew him well misses him he was made of something better than the usual stuff. Like you-

I will give Mrs S your message I pity Johnnie very much I suppose the war is the same as usual. "The allies are shot" still like Lonigan.

How is the cold weather agreeing with you? I hardly ever stir out except to go to mass we have snow rain & sleet every day I hope the weather will be better than that for you come you might make strange with it. I am glad you enjoyed the plays but the tears surprised me for a man. I thought such things belonged to the females you can cry for me as I don't ever cry. I have no news this time

    So goodbye with all my best love
    Your ever loving

    May

39 Belgrave Square
Rathmines
Dublin
15th Feby, 1916

My dearest May,
    Your letter today was a great pleasure as usual but somehow I was disappointed that it was so short. I suppose that was due to the natural upset at home on Tim's leaving to make his

fortune. I hope the poor chap will get on well anyhow and will reconcile himself to the queer people of Mitchelstown better than you did. I'm afraid you wouldn't get on well in business. You would be too fond of telling people your frank opinion of them. I hope it will never come to that between you and me. Somehow or another for the past few days I have been feeling depressed – maybe it's the worries in the office that have been affecting me without my knowing it so I hope that you will, like the dear little girl that you are, send me a nice loving letter in the next few days to cheer me up. Now amn't I a selfish beast to be telling you all this to worry you but somehow I can't help letting you know. However there's a good time coming on Saturday week and I am sure that I will be quite cured of the dumps by then.

I'm not surprised to hear about the bad weather you're having in the country. One of the men in my office was away in the south (Cork) for the past few days and he tells me that the country all down there is covered with snow. We haven't had any in Dublin but the weather has been very cold and wet some days. Today is wet and stormy and I got nearly wet through coming home from the office.

Moll went out to Kingstown on Sunday evening and started work in the Post Office there yesterday morning. We have been expecting a line from her since but haven't heard anything yet. I expect she will like it very well though as both the work and the town are all right. There's a good deal of talk all round at present about the coming of peace but it impossible to say what chance there is of it. I hope to God something may come of all the talk soon for I don't know how the middle classes- never to speak of the unfortunate poor in the towns and cities – are going to hang on if the war lasts for another year or so. The country people are lucky that needn't worry about taxes or increased prices. Well, love, I have spun this letter out without saying anything pleasant or interesting and maybe have added to your worries by it. If I have will you please forgive me and let me off for this time. I won't offend again. With all my warmest love to my darling girl from her ever loving and constant

James

Togherstown
Ballinea
16th Feb 1916

My own dearest James,

I was indeed glad to get your letter I was not sure if you would fulfil the promise you gave the day before in your note, by the way I must thank you for sending that bit of a note when when (sic) you had not time to write I was delighted to find busy and all as you were you did not disappoint me I was very sorry you did not think my last letter just as I meant it to be but I was really upset with Tim going & Mother so worried you under stood that still you were annoyed & you knowing so well my intentions were the best However I hope by this time that my own darling little man has got over that dumpy feeling for me I am in the best of spirits & have not felt better this long while.

Tim landed quiet (sic) safely under the protection of a big Kerry man a cattle jobber who put him into his car at Knocklong. & promised to see him the next time he went to Mitchelstown you say I would not get on well at business will you wonder when I tell you all the people I met when down there made great enquiries about me & gave me all sorts of good wishes etc that shows I sup-pose that I hid my feeling of their dislike very well you are wrong there now James about my giving my frank opinion of people to themselves I never do for instance that mother Joseph did not know I was fond of her until I was near finished in Ferbane- don't you remember me telling you how she said it was hard to un-derstand me for a long time-you must not understand I should conclude from you getting downhearted over my letter still I know you do from many & many other things about telling you what I think of you. Why do you say you hope it will never come to that with us? I have told you long ago. If not in words I did in giving you my hand & heart the very day you asked it what I know I would not have done with any other. I would have taken ever so long to consider & surely consult my Mother but you know I did neither, that showed the seed of affection had been sown, much less opinion. I will say no more now except renew my best love to my own dear James

From May

National Health Insurance Commission (Ireland)
Pembroke house
Upper Mount Street
Dublin
18ʰ Feby, 1916

My own darling,
Well your letter this morning was a breath of Spring all right so I can start this by saying how grateful I am to you and how thankful to God for the great blessing of my sweet girl's

affection. I know better than anyone can how cranky and sore headed I am ordinarily and for that reason I distrust myself very much for fear that some time or another something may happen between us two which will offend you or make you doubt my love for you. I have already said it to you many times so that you must be sick of hearing it that I can never get over what ever made you think of me out of the ordinary. The constant proofs you have given me however of your regard make me very happy but they reproach me also as seeming to take them too much as a matter of course. For example I ought to know very well that your deciding straight off the very first day I spoke to you was a tremendous instance of confidence and of regard. I am afraid that I have taken that a bit too coolly but my own mind had been bent in that direction for so long that I could hardly realise properly what a difficult thing it was in the case of the other party to the bargain to decide straight off. However I had some faint glimmer of the difficulty and I am sure you will do me the justice of remembering that I was anxious that day for you to take time to reflect on the matter. In any case, dearest, I do love you very much for the marks of confidence and regards you have given me and with your help I hope, if God spares me, to make you happy and to be a good husband to you. I was glad to hear that Tim got to his destination safely and amused to see that he was making friends so soon. How did he get on with the Kerry jobber? Perhaps he was an old acquaintance owing to Tim's long connection with the cattle trade at fairs etc!

The weather is rotten today and promises to be the same for the weekend. I hope it will improve a bit before next Saturday when I am hoping to see you. If I'm not too busy next week I shall probably take Saturday off and come down Friday evening. Would you prefer that or that I should wait until Saturday. Perhaps if I waited till Saturday I might meet you in Mullingar and be home with you. About this time last year the dance was in Mullingar. Had you any idea then of what would happen in the year. I had a very strong notion anyhow that I'd chance my arm whatever might come of it before the year was out. Have no news at all worth relating. Accountant[35] is away for past few days so I'm running the show on my own. Give my regards to all and with ever faithful and con-

stant love for your dear self
From darling May's little man
James
[By the way I forgot to say that my remarks about your being
likely to tell me some time or other what you thought of me were
entirely a joke and were not seriously meant. So please don't
worry about them and don't take everything I say so dreadfully
seriously,
Your loving
James]

Togherstown
Ballinea
19th Feb 1916

My dearest James,
                    I was very glad to get your letter this morning early
in comparison with other mornings as Mother, Laddy & Nano &
Mrs Seery were at mass don't think by that I am losing my bit of
religion for I had to stay at home to mind my brother that's the
way I'll be staying at home to mind somebody else very soon.
Who is that unfortunate somebody? While I talk of religion Nora
was inquiring to Mrs S. about a prayer book she lost perhaps you
would have it in the pocket of your over coat I might have had
it the first Sunday I was up It was your Mother's I had the last Sunday I hope she will get it, rather soon to blacken my character you
know.
This is a glorious day real spring not one about the place all gone
to a ploughing match Joe Finn[36] is taking part he was all excited
had his <u>boots polished</u>, nothing else he expects to win but if he
doesn't he has lost his days hire & 2/6 fee that will be awful I hope
he'll get something anyway. Christy is selling cattle to day, he is
gone off to see Seery's sold so we don't know what has he got or
did he sell at all.
I might be in Mullingar next Sat. I could wait for your train that
will be grand I never told Mrs Seery when you intended coming but I will tonight if she comes up. She (Mrs S) had the Misses
Kelly down on Wed. Pauline Aggie & Rose[37] the latter is going
to some job in England crying how Jim listed etc. he sold all her

> # The Irishmen in the Trenches are calling for YOU.
>
> ---
>
> ## Ask yourself squarely whether you are justified in turning a deaf ear to THEM.
>
> ---
>
> **Apply for particulars of Allowances, etc., at local Recruiting Office.**

rings while he was with her even the wedding of course they don't intend going near the bride Mrs Kiernan says she won't either. This Kerry jobber only got acquainted with Christy going along on the train to Clara, T would have gone further only the big man was charmed with the child. I am sure Tim did not half like being called a <u>child</u>. I have no other news so I will say good bye with my very best love. It won't be long now until you are down. I hope this weather will continue, I feel this day doing me good

Warmest love to dear James from his loving big May

National Health Insurance Commission (Ireland)
Pembroke house
Upper Mount Street
Dublin
19th Feby 1916

My dearest girl,

I must keep my promise that you should have a letter tomorrow but I am pretty afraid I shall not be able to make it very interesting as I have absolutely no news at all to relate. Luckily I won't be in the same difficulty next week as I presume you will not insist on my sending you a letter from Lockardstown to Togherstown on Sunday next. I am looking forward very keenly to my visit as I'm dying to see you. How is the ankle getting on since you went home. I suppose all right now that you have such a lazy time as you say you have.

We are expecting Moll home tomorrow for a few hours. It's grand for her to be so near now, she can come home any time she pleases. My mother had a note from her during the week. She finds both the town and the staff in the office very pleasant so we are all hoping she will get on well.

On re-reading your letter (I always read them about 20 times) I was sorry to see that your mother and yourself were so worried about Tim. Of course it's hard lines that he should have to go so far away at his age but all the same he's amongst his own to a certain extent and Jennie & himself will be great company to each other Besides there are plenty at home in any case to keep your mother company and it's a good job for any young chap to stir out early if he has to earn his own living. I see too many cases here in town of fellows living on their parents up to 20 and 25 years of age and then trying for rotten clerks jobs in Government Departments at 25/- or 30/- a week. That reminds me that I have been enquiring about Johnnie in a few places but up to the present without success. It's the devil entirely to get jobs for men clerks at present; the women are taking the bread out of all our mouths[38] but I'm still hoping that I may succeed. Pity he's not hearing anything from Cork. I thought that was pretty well a dead cert. Tell Mrs Seery that I am making further efforts and I will write to her early next week. Today is a great improvement on yesterday. It's very bright and pleasant but very cold. I'm writing this in the office and the fire is gone out as well as all the staff (Saturday afternoon) so I'm afraid you won't be able to read it my hands are so cold. I must close now. One of the beautiful charwomen put her head in just now so I must go. She is evidently wondering what the hell is keeping me in and she wanting to clean up the room. In any case I want my dinner and I know you wouldn't come between a hungry man and his food. So goodbye my dearest love for the present. Hope to have a letter from my darling girl tomorrow. With fondest love and kisses

From your loving
James

31 Belgrave Square
Rathmines
Dublin
20th Feby 1916

My Darling May

You won't get this letter tomorrow so you will have to live off the fat of the letter you get to-day. (I hope you got it by the way) until Thursday. I ought to have written today in time for post but I got lazy after dinner (gluttony I expect) and so put off writing until it was too late.

The post by the way goes very early from here now (owing to war economies like everything else) - about 4 o'clock so one has to be very brisk to get to the post at all on Sundays. I expect that's why the letter you posted home this day fortnight (how long ago it seems) didn't reach in time. I fact it's a struggle for me any day to write to you during the day at the office as I am constantly being interrupted by callers, men coming to submit cases for decision &c &c, and if I defer it until the rush is over it is too lat. So now admit I am a good little man to write so regularly especially as I have always been a rotten hand at writing letters. I always envy the people who can dash off pleasant chatty entertaining letters without any apparent trouble. Both Nora and Moll are great at that job, so is Baby Finn (my cousin) and you're a very good hand at it yourself too. Whereas in my case after I have exhausted the "taking my pen in hand to write to you these few lines hoping you are well" and then fall back on the weather I'm stumped. I gave your message about the prayer book to Nora. She has been running around like a clucking hen for the past week or so since she lost it. I cleared you character with her but I think she blames Mrs Seery now. Anyhow she's quite sure it's between you it is, so you'd both better bring your own payer books the next time you come up. Glad to hear you're not losing your religion anyway. The unfortunate somebody you refer to is thinking the day will never come when you take him in charge. You'll have a heavy handful I'm afraid, but not as heavy I hope as Rose Duffy. The more you wipe your boots on some girls, the more they love you. It's a curious kind of temperament I must say. There ought to be a limit to forbearance in such a case as Jim Duffy's. Well love, I

think the work in the office will ease off this week all right and I'll probably be able to get a few days off next week. If you are going to Mullingar on Saturday I suppose you would prefer me to wait until that day. Either Friday or Saturday will probably be all the same to me. Thanks for tip about Mrs Seery but I hadn't forgotten to write to her. Shall do so tomorrow and she will have on Monday same time as you have this. Moll was in today for a few hours from Kingstown. She is charmed with both the office and the lodgings and will I'm sure be very happy. I suppose you have hardly had time to hear from Tim yet. Give my regards to your mother, Nano and the boys. Hope my namesake pulled off the first prize at the ploughing for the credit of the family name. As usual I have no news at all. Everything goes on ...as usual here not like the country where something is always happening. Dublin life is much duller I think or maybe it is I'm a dull dog myself. Well goodbye now my dearest love with warmest love until I see you,
    Your loving James

Togherstown
Ballinea
Sunday (postmarked 21 feb?)

Puzzle- find the kisses five
    My dearest James,
        Y●ou are indeed a very very good boy to think of me for Sunday I was very glad to get letter but I will have better next Sunday Please God. We met Mrs Kiernan at mass she was going that eve to call on the bride for curiosity will there be many calling on us for curiosity I wonder. But the best news of the day- Johnnie had a letter from a fellow in Pims saying the clerk's job was certain when the directors meet on the 29th Feb. It will be grand if he gets it Mrs S & himself are gone to B●allymore today & mother & Christy to Mearescourt (Wynne's)
I am after being on one of the corporal works of charity, down seeing Essy & Paddy Nolan. They are suffering from colds & mumps and so I have special sympathy for them. Mrs Nolan came too. She read with me so I brought her in and showed her my ring- fancy that to be the second time for her to be in the house She did not adopt(?) any of Jack's curiosity she was here before when Jennie was getting married, of course there was no

luck she did not wish me.

About the ploughing match- Joe only took third prize 10/- It was better than nothing but he was very indignant when the decisions were given he declared he could plough with any of them when he came home he told my mother he took first & they wouldn't give it to him. Favour(?) in Hell he says, none of this would be heard only he got a few bottles of stout to make him brave he is in a grate (sic) state about pigs he has to sell afraid anyone else would get a better price than him for comrade pigs I am sure you are taking a great interest in these things you will be sorry to hear Mrs Tinog(?) Thomson[39] of Nugent's Cross roads gave a wedding party for her daughter, all the invited guests did not turn up so she is giving another spree next Sat to give them all a chance, very kind of her- Christy sold his cattle yesterday £21-10 he got, he was pleased I think. T Seery got £21 and he was saying before his cattle were better than ours so I don't know which were the best ours were seen at an advantage in the <> their _father_ that might have something to do with it but sure the _poor widow_ wanted the 10/- worse than Mrs S that was the whole of it I suppose.

Did you know Larry Cunningham one of his sisters, an old girl of Ned Seery[40] is going to be•married to a fellow the name of Duncan there are a lot of marriages spoken of; Jocie Dardis[41] she was at the nursing for a while is to be married to a Tom Manley I don't think do you know either party, your mother might.

How did you think of asking for my ankle• you will only make me pettish like the children if you take notice of me like that I seldom feel it now. It must have only been at started a bit.

Ned Seery is going very fast after Lizzie Fox, they are telling me but I'd get it hard to believe it. They say she meets him etc. Mike Killian went so far as to say she is getting fond of him (Ned S). Tommy is still constant & true. Johnnie does not seem to have seen anything to suit in the country.

I won't say any more now afraid it would be taxed so I will wind up with the usual amount of love from your •loving

   May

National Health Insurance Commission (Ireland)
Pembroke house
Upper Mount Street
Dublin
22nd Feby 1916

My darling girl,
Today again I am afraid I must put you off with a very short letter. I have been extremely hard pushed all day and am writing now under pressure in order to catch the post. Since I finished that last sentence I have been twice interrupted so I hope you will sympathise with my sad case. Since you're talking of pettishness, I may say I'm as fond of sympathy as any child so from all points of view you'll have a hard time with me when you have to put up with me every day for the remainder of our natural lives. My mother had a letter from Mrs Seery this morning letting us know the good news about Johnnie. We were all delighted on his account and hope he starts on his new job soon and that he will have the best of luck in it.

I failed to keep my promise to you to write to her yesterday but I must try and manage a minute or two now to write her a line. I suppose I had better say that I will go down on Saturday and that I will meet you in Mullingar. I was amused to hear that Mrs John Duffy is only an object of curiosity in the country now. I expect we'll be the same presently but that they will all be coming to see me and not you as the object of curiosity to see what you could see in me to induce you to marry me.

Glad to hear about all the romances. You can trust me to keep a quiet tongue in my head about them all. I haven't the pleasure of knowing Miss Fox's appearance but I expect she's good looking all right or Ned wouldn't be after her. How about your own brothers? They ought to be on the warpath soon if they take after their sisters who are all early birds[42]. By the way, thanks for kisses which I succeeded in finding although in one or two cases you were mean enough to try to hide them by blots. That was hardly fair was it? Hope I won't have so much difficulty next time in getting the real thing.

I have been again three times interrupted since I wrote page 1 so I will bring this rambling epistle to a close. In fact I'm so bothered and worried just at the moment that I don't know what I have

written so will you please, like a darling, forgive me. Probably I'll
write again tomorrow. With my warmest love to my own darling
and with heaps of kisses
From her loving
James

Mullingar

Togherstown
Ballinea
Mullingar
23rd Feb 1916

My dearest James
      I know I am horrid not to have written to you yesterday
you are so good to write and you so very busy always but I intended writing only I had a bad head ache & went to bed with it
I slept until I missed a chance of posting you can know it is not
always easy to post here messengers sometimes are very scarce.
But it's not what you would call cute of me to tell I would go to
bed with only a head ache but I'm not one to be fond of lying
up with anything whatever gives me that bad head ache I don't
know it was not the winter gardens this time However I must
thank God they are few and far between. I feel quite fresh after

it today and always do I never was as much ashamed as I was to have to go to bed that night in your house. I had to do it I would never have gone. I'm sure your mother thought it very –well pettish if you like, what matter now if she never thinks worse of me than that I'm very safe.

Joe Finn has come from the fair he got not what he expected but beat us by 5/- that was a consolation to him Christy got £5.10 each for 5 five pigs but gave most of it back again for a fat pig, there were great prices got but I don't think people were satisfied.

Mattee Keanan[43] the black smith was going round with his love letters Sunday I was not at home but he was asking Mrs S. about "us" he said he thought you'd be a priest long ago, he used to be serving mass with you long ago, he gave you great praise says it's a "prince" you ought to be married so now.-

Tim is getting on grand he wrote to us & to Mrs Seery. Jennie's little boy got jealous when he saw Tim & left. She will get it very hard to get another.

I will be in Mullingar Sat so will my Mother but she will go home in the sim(?). I expect & I will wait for somebody to bring me home I suppose I'll get a seat from whoever comes to meet you. I have no more news so I will say bye-bye to my own little man (rather soon to be holding such a grip on you)

very very best love to my dear James from his loving
May

National Health Insurance Commission (Ireland)
Pembroke house
Upper Mount Street
Dublin
24th Feby 1916

My dearest girl,

You needn't have been so penitent about not writing to me yesterday. I really didn't expect to hear from you and in any case I know very well that it is not always easy to get letters posted in Togherstown. I was very sorry indeed to hear that the real cause of your not writing was a recurrence of the headache you had at my place. I hope that my poor darling wasn't so bad as she was then. I pitied you very much that last evening you had the headache because I could see very well that you weren't really able to sit up. I'm quite sure my mother didn't think you pettish for going to bed: you were quite right to go. I was glad to hear that Joe beat the Fays with his pigs – for the credit of the family name. I think Christy must have sold his too cheap especially if his "piebald" was one of the lot. I'm sure the piebald would go much more than £5:10:0 as a curiosity for the waxworks in Henry Street. He'd be a great attraction along with the "fat woman" and the "bear lady". I was very pleased to hear of the good opinion that Matty Keanan has of me. If I get many more "flowers" thrown at me like that I'll begin to fancy myself too much. I'm beginning to think now that you were a fortunate ~~little~~ <u>big</u> girl to get hold of such a treasure. So you'd better keep your nose very clean and be particularly nice to me (and <u>above all</u> don't refuse me kisses) or I'll go back on you. So now mind yourself. Glad to hear Tim is getting on so well and hope he will continue so. I wrote to Mrs. Seery on Friday to let her know I'd be down Saturday evening. Perhaps she would come herself to the station to meet us if you suggest it. If not I suppose that the <u>Fays</u> are going to meet us and between the two houses we should have to walk. I don't care "tuppence" myself but I don't suppose you would enjoy stumping from Castletown. In fact I'd much prefer walking if I had you to myself. I don't think I'll write tomorrow as probably you'd be gone to the station on Saturday before a letter could arrive. I have nothing else to say now except to send my dearest and most devoted love as usual. I shall live for the next two days on the expectation of Saturday. By the way, I didn't sleep last night till 2 o'clock thinking about you

Warmest love again my darling girl
James

..No sign of the work easing off here but I'll take a few days off next week anyhow and to h—with everybody. James

Togherstown
Ballinea
Mullingar
25th Feb 1916

My dearest James
I was very glad to get your letter this morn. I was looking out for it and happened to be at the window up stairs when Mrs

L was coming down the hill & it teeming snow. I could scarcely
believe my eye when I saw she got down on her knees & crept
out on the creep hole, you know the hole for the sheep so it is no
wonder the poor thing looked so dilapidated. I hope it will never
come to that with me but I'd make you go around with the letters
& I'd keep the stirabout hot till you would come home.
We had a letter from Jennie today, Tim is not a bit lonely up very
early studying she said he had a letter from Joe Tyrell, the boy
that was going to Mullingar, along with a very nice letter she gave
us one piece out of it. It was this-I was very lonely for you but I
have you forgotten now, be sure & don't let much of the year go
by without writing to me I'll be looking out for your letter
Jack Nolan was here today he was killing a pig very much inclined
to inquire about your property etc. You know Jack
It will be all right about the car I'll take good care not to have to
walk I'm very lazy as far as walking goes
Goodbye now till tomorrow when I will have pleasure of seeing
my poor hard working little man All my best love to my dearest
James from May
   Excuse this horrid letter I'm cold & hurried
   May

Rathmines

Togherstown
Ballinea
Mullingar
3rd March 1916

My dearest James
    I got your letters today & yesterday alright I can tell you I was very glad to get them to brighten me up I have been in low spirits since Sat I got neuralgy (sic) a continual num (sic) pain over my right eye with a very frequent sting from a broken tooth I slept each night between the stings you know the way they take you I have a gum bill (sic) now & I hope as it gets bigger this nagging pain will go I have not got any trouble with my teeth this last six months but all the time I lived in dread of them the only thing is they are no serious harm.

Like yourself I am looking forward to your visit at Easter but I don't know what to say to my visit to the city I'm not going to go now between this & Easter & by the time you are gone back after Easter it will be only a month from that until the 1st of June & a month is very short passing in preparation for something very pleasant to think of & I expect to be very busy I was consulting my Mother yesterday she said it would be a very foolish trip so near our marriage & having people talking (perhaps say you were trying to back out of it) Don't think me awful now to be changing my mind but I did not realize how near we were to our marriage at Easter neither did you I think-if you saw me nearer than a month of our own marriage there would be no novelty at all in getting married, but if nothing turns up to prevent me I will go to the races I hope you won't be disgusted with this changing but it is hard to decide on anything until it is almost at hand

You are very good to be thinking of giving me something to show how you love me but indeed I have proof enough You should not be giving yourself the trouble in case you did tho' I would like a pair of gloves any sort I'm not very particular About being nice to you at Easter of course I will a vic[44] but sure I'm always nice- too nice for my peace of mind

I have not a word of news. Yes Tom Macken Marlinstown will probably with Francis O'Neill[45]. Your Mother may know the gent I think, I will conclude with fondest & warmest love to my dearest James

from your old girl May

The break in the weather was a great disappointment to the farmers in general

My dearest James

[written on envelope]

I had this letter written yesterday & could not get to post it. I was very glad this morn to hear my name called out for a letter I was in bed & got out & ran down in my dressing gown- lazy girl you will say- but I have got a lot of my teeth & I feel tired & weak my face is swollen & very sore today still I am on the mend T.G[46]. I hope you won't be vexed when you see by enclosed letter that I have given up the thought of going to Dublin & that I intend to go to the races not that I prefer to go to the races but just that I might see you, perhaps you cannot go tho' on account of the Accountant being gone to London -would he not be vexed with you for not going with him? If I thought you would get tired of me as soon as I pretend I did I would not get over it that easy. Indeed such a thought never crossed my mind. If it did you would be apt to hear more about too

Mrs Seery had a long letter today from Jim Finn & he is wishing he was on the bog road these fine days & she told me to ask you is your uncle Frank gone yet & how is Baby is she still on sick leave & tell your Mother she (Mrs S) is busy but will write soon

I have no news at all so I will say goodbye with fondest & warmest love from your ever-loving

May

Don't bother about me at Easter I mean about bring me anything

National Health Commission (Ireland)
Pembroke House
Upper Mount Street
Dublin
6/3/1916

My darling,

I have only time to write a line to let you know I got back all right. I haven't had time yet to get lonesome because I have been very much rushed and so have not been able to think. I hope however that I won't be so very lonely because after all I have had the divil's luck ever to get you and so I ought to be contented. I haven't seen any one at home yet so I can't tell you what has happened since I left. I didn't see any sign of a bridal party at Broadstone[47] when I got out so I don't know how the rice got into the train. Hope you got through your business all right and that you weren't too lonely when I left.

I'm sure you're too good and too sensible to worry over such "silly" matters. You know you often told me not to be "silly" so I must try and be very sensible for the next couple of months. When you're writing let me know how Christie is going on. He seems to be worrying a bit himself over his mysterious ailment. I shall probably drop into Hopkins[48] tomorrow to see after wristlet watch and you will probably have it before the end of the week. With my warmest and most devoted love to my dear girl.

> *Ever your fond*
> *James*

Mullingar
6th March 1916

My dearest James

A moment to tell you not to be lonely at all at all, it's not worth while you will soon see too much of me I hope you gave my love to Mother, Nora & Moll. Now be a very good boy & I'll pray & fast for you during the Lent if I can at all I hope that we have pleasant weather- this day is lovely. Hope no one will touch you for breaking the eggs. Tell me if they do.

> *Very very, very best love from*
> *May*

National Health Commission (Ireland)
Pembroke House
Upper Mount Street
Dublin
7/3/1916

My dearest love,

Thank you ever so much for your dear note received this morning. I can only find the time to scribble a line to say how much it has pleased and comforted me. I know very well you will remember to pray for me that I may eventually become somewhat more fitted to be your husband. I always feel that nothing could be half good enough for my dear little wife-to-be. I haven't been a bit lonely since I came back although I have been thinking about you constantly. I think there is something warm round my heart at present which keeps me comforted and in good spirits, although I must certainly say that I should dearly like to see you if only for a moment. I hardly think I shall ever see too much of you, I can't imagine at present how I could possibly do so.

I had a very tragic reminder today or rather yesterday of the uncertainty of life. A man named Culhane who was up to a couple of years ago the solicitor to our Department here died suddenly from a clot of blood- I suppose on the brain. A young man only 35 years and with a fine job. He was Taxing Master in the Four Courts with £1000 a year. I heard it as a rumour yesterday when I got back to

DEATH OF MASTER J. F. CULHANE

The death occurred rather suddenly yesterday morning at his residence in Rathmines of Mr. John F. Culhane, Taxing Master at the Four Courts. The cause of death is said to have been the development of a clot of blood. Deceased, who was very popular, was aged only 35, and always seemed to enjoy vigorous health. He became a solicitor in 1904, and was appointed Taxing Master in 1914, having previously been solicitor to the Irish Insurance Commissioners.

As a mark of respect to deceased's memory, the other Taxing Masters adjourned their respective courts without proceeding with the business listed for the day. Deceased was married to a daughter of Mr. D. Sheehy, M.P., and took an active part in the election in South Co. Dublin, in which Ald. Cotton, U.I., achieved a signal success.

Irish Independent March 7 1916

the office but was inclined to discredit it. I knew him very well and was rather friendly with him while he was our solicitor. So you see what a chancy job you are taking on in marrying me. No news at all. No one beat me for breaking the eggs. There were only two cracked so I escaped. In any case I threatened you on them.

with my warmest and undying love
your devoted James

Togherstown
Ballinea
Mullingar
7thMarch 1916

My dearest James
     You were indeed very thoughtfull (sic) to manage a moment to send me a line, I must say you are a very good dear man. I was very glad to have your letter this morn and very early I had it too, but I could not find energy to get through my few jobs having nothing to hurry for better than dinner, for the first time I felt a want in country life but I was not so silly as I call it as to let that be seen but I hurried to write this letter to you and then set to & make <u>pancakes</u> for the tea on account of Shrove Tuesday, it is a big job for so many but I wish there was one more. I fancy you would not care for them- I will eat them tho' I know well I will wish I did not –Johnnie C. did not hear anything today Christy is not feeling well he is staying inside all day & complains of pains in his side he got a bottle of pills & ointment. I hope they will have the desired effect -nothing wrong with his appetite yet- he was anxious to know if the eggs were dropping out on you. I did not tell Mrs S, I was afraid she would say I had a right to mind them, she was up as usual last night, gave me "down the banks" for not telling her anything. I told her to ask me some suitable questions & I'd see if I could answer. She said I was too clever altogether for her taste I don't know why she thinks me like that but she has hinted that way very often of late what harm I'm sure you would like to have a clever girl for your <u>wife</u>, here is no news at all going around that is worth writing. Joe Nolan was here yesterday evening but I know you are old sick of his sayings &etc. Jennie wrote to Mrs S today. She seems to be getting on grand I got back in the two train I had not one minute to spare. I hope you were not lonely last night when you went home I was

very lonely sitting at the fire not but Mrs S said I did not even say if they were or not when I went to bed it was relieved by tears & then away with me to dreamland no such luck as happy dreams even.

I have not another word now but
Very very best love from your own
big girl May

[I am childish enough to be quiet (sic) looking forward to getting watch, not the watch so much as the token of love it must be, at least that it is in my eyes.

Love from
May

National Health Commission (Ireland)
Pembroke House
Upper Mount Street
Dublin
8/3/1916

I was delighted and pleased with your letter this morning. It has kept my heart ringing all day up to the present for it is clear all through it that you are not quite the superior " sensible" thing that you were trying to humbug me into believing.. It is the greatest possible comfort and happiness to me to know that my dear girl thinks of me so much and so highly. I suppose it's heartless to be glad to hear that you had recourse to tears on Monday night. Is this the superior girl that never cried and who was so contemptuous of me for being "silly" when I thought I was only affectionate? Well I am glad to see that you were moved to tears on my account and I love you all the more dearly (if that is possible) for it. For my part, I'm not a bit inclined to cry these days. In fact I feel quite pleased with myself and inclined to shake myself by the hand- almost indeed to stand myself a drink- because I have been so lucky as to get such a treasure as your love. The thought of it warms and comforts me so that I can almost feel something warm and singing within me all day long. I didn't have any pancakes for tea yesterday evening so I'd have done better in more ways than one if I had been able to help you to eat yours. I suppose everyone forgot it at home and indeed I forgot it myself till I got your letter this morning. That's one of the advantages of being young like you; you don't forget the pleasant cus-

toms of the children.

Sorry to hear Mrs Seery has been worrying you over your secrets. I don't know why she should think you have any. The only thing between you and me is that we love each other dearly and I expect everyone can guess that pretty well (in my case anyhow) without being told it. I'm not surprised that she thinks you're pretty clever although I hope she doesn't think you "smart" in the bad sense. I have certainly always thought you a young girl of remarkable character and intelligence and goodness, far beyond your very youthful years, and I am all the more delighted that I hooked the prize. What a dear sweet clever little <u>wife</u> I shall have one of these fine days! Well my dearest love, about the watch, I called into Hopkins yesterday and selected a couple of wristlet watches which I thought would suit. O'Leary, the manager, recommended both strongly and said he would get them going for a day or two to see which one was the better. They are at present racing against each other under his supervision and he will let me know on <u>Friday</u> which I should take. I shall send the watch on <u>Friday evening</u> so that you may have it in good time for Sunday or if you like I can get him to send you a selection of two or three on approval. Let me know would you prefer this. I shall probably not write tomorrow but will wait until I send watch on Friday. No news at all except that I am getting back into harness very well and am quite happy knowing that you love me. Thanks ever so much for the kisses which I return even more heartily than they were given.

With all my dearest and warmest love and blessings to my darling from your future husband, James

Togherstown
Ballinea
Mullingar
9[th]March 1916

My dearest James
Very many thanks for your nice letter of this morning. I was very pleased to see by it you are keeping in such spirits. I am in the best of form now I was at Mass Ash Wed. Mass only because I'm keeping my loaded conscience for a Mullingar priest if I can manage the point without anyone knowing it.-About the

The Exact
DUBLIN TIME
AT
HOPKINS & HOPKINS
The Waltham Watch Depot,
DUBLIN,
Who have now installed a direct time cable with
GREENWICH OBSERVATORY.

DUBLIN TIME   LONDON TIME

Hopkins & Hopkins was a fine jeweller on Sackville Street

watch I think it would be better only send the one. I will rely on
your taste I will be very anxious to have it for Sunday, just today
I had an invitation for myself & Christy to spend Sunday eve with
Mary Kelly Castletown. I dare say the bridegroom will be there &
of course I will swank it before them as it may be the last time I'll
ever see that party I did not want to go at all but Mother said it
would look bad to fall black out people talk so much.

We had a letter from Jennie today she was full of the weddings
that took place , the last day there were five going on all day
the last one in the evening the groom came galloping like the
D- (Jennie told me give you the hint) & all the cars after followed
by a carriage with the bride & brides made (sic) they came back
with the horse last, best man mounted & the carriage first with
bride & groom, one man came running into Jack Healy an hour
before his marriage for a ring, couldn't get one to fit in the town,
that's what would have happen (sic) with us if we had rushed it,
you would be running to Fox's & the forge's workshop trying to
get me fitted. Christy was in bed nearly all day yesterday, he is
up today and seems to feel much better. Mrs Seery is very very
anxious about Johnnie a bit vexed with him too that he's not
more anxious, he went to Ballymore Tuesday & did not come
back since to see if a letter had turned up, she is afraid he got in
with Dan Kiernan or someone like that, the Cork affair looks very
bad. Mrs S got a fancy match box in Tommy's possession a present from his girl of course, big oak with harps & shamrock on it.
Mother was telling the lads today not to forget the Novena for
the speedy end of the war to St Patrick, Christy said no such thing
for when the war is over he is beggared- I have no news now so
I'll conclude with my best love & very best love to my dear James
from his loving

    May

Write to Mrs Seery – she had a letter from your mother. She said
that Father Moran said we would be six months married before
we'd know she was in the house & she was bound to be neglected
intentional or otherwise; I think she feels a bit down hearted
some way & I hope that feeling will not grow on her or my account.

Bye Bye now I hope I have the watch in time to swank before M

Kelly if that's not silly but I would not be that sort with anyone only her
   Your loving "big girl"
   May]

National Health Commission (Ireland)
Pembroke House
Upper Mount Street
Dublin
9/3/1916

   My dearest love,
      Although I said yesterday I would not write today I am doing so now. I called to Hopkins today about watch and as the watch I selected was doing well (it had kept quite correct time since Thursday) I thought I might as well let my dear girl have it at once. It is going off today and I hope that you will like it. The bracelet is a spring one so I think you will have no difficulty about getting it on. If there is anything wrong or any little thing you would like changed let me know and I will see to it at once. Have not got much time at my disposal so will you please forgive me if I do not say much this time. In any case I have really nothing worth saying beyond sending you my undying love as usual. With warmest love to my dearest and with fervent kisses
   Always your loving and devoted
   James
X X X X X X X X X X X X X X X X X X
Is that enough?? I think I'd take your breath away if I went so hard on you as that and I suppose I will do that someday. May it be soon!!
   James

National Health Commission (Ireland)
Pembroke House
Upper Mount Street
Dublin
11/3/1916

   My ever dearest darling,
      I was more disgusted and disappointed this morning than I can explain when I saw from your letter that you had not received the watch. Hopkins' people made it up in a box in my presence on Thursday and sealed it for dispatch <u>at once</u> to the post. They wouldn't let me take it myself as they assured me that

it would go off <u>without delay</u>. This was at 3 o'clock and I can't understand why you should not have got it yesterday morning without fail especially as it was registered. I trust however it has turned up this morning. I was so anxious <u>yesterday</u> that there should be no hitch that when I got your letter saying you had been invited to Mary Kelly's I called up O'Leary, the manager, on the telephone and questioned him closely as to whether the watch had <u>certainly</u> gone off all right on Thursday. I am very much annoyed over it, especially as I wanted to give you the pleasure of the surprise in getting it a day sooner than you had expected. I hope I may have a note from you in the morning to say that it arrived all right. You say that you are anxious to have the watch for a reason that I can guess. Well you can understand how anxious I am that you should have it for the very same reason, that I love my dearest girl above and far beyond anything else in this world. I'm not ashamed to say that to you although you seem to be shy of saying the same. Still I hope that it is true although you don't say it. Thanks, love for the kisses. You wouldn't ask "who is good in the holy season to send them". I know very well that my dear sweet girl is always good so that I hope you won't expect me to take too seriously the references to loaded consciences and sin and all the rest of it. I imagine the priest must have a job to keep from laughing sometimes when he hears your "sins".

I was very much amused to hear about the rush of marriages in Mitchelstown. I don't imagine our case would have been so bad if we had suddenly taken the sweet madness of getting married last week. Anyhow the hurry and little difficulties of that sort add to the pleasant romance and the dear happiness of carrying off your own little wife almost by main force and marrying her out of hand. The more I think of it, the more I'm sorry I didn't do it so there's no use your trying to frighten me by horrible examples from Mitchelstown. I taxed my mother with what you told me about Father Moran and she only laughed so I don't think she is inclined to be too downhearted over our marriage. I feel quite sure that you and she will get on famously and will grow to like each other more the more you see of each other.

Of course it's not always easy for two people to live together

day in day out without little quarrels (I suppose even you and
I will quarrel sometimes-I know I have a rather sullen temper)
but I think you are both two sweet-tempered to be out for very
long. With God's blessing we will all live happy and contented
together and when I get out of temper, I hope I will always think
of the sweet trustfulness and confidence so freely shown to me
by the dear girl who gave herself to me in the first flower of her
youth and beauty. Now that may sound a bit high flowing but
it is all, my darling, true and sincere and heartfelt. Glad to hear
that Christy is doing so well. Give my regards to your mother,
Nano and all. I send you a thousand kisses and warmest and most
heartfelt love.
    Yours for ever & ever
    James

National Health Commission (Ireland)
Pembroke House
Upper Mount Street
Dublin
13/3/1916

    My dearest love,
        I was delighted to see by your letter of yesterday that you
were pleased with the watch and with my taste in the selection.
As a matter of fact my one regret in the matter is that I couldn't
afford to buy you one much more in keeping with my love for
you. As regards my taste being better in the watch than in the
wife, I wish to remark (as Bret Harte would say) that anyone
could get that same watch or a better one any day in the week
for a few pounds whereas there is only one May Fay and money
couldn't buy her. She was fool enough to sell herself (or rather
give herself away) without properly realising her own value.
That's why I shall always be inclined to reproach myself for taking
you at a mean disadvantage because you were too innocent to
value yourself enough and foolish enough to value me too highly.
However as I have already said in my last letter I do love and honour you to the best of my poor power for your dear goodness and
sweetness and with God's help I'll try to manage so that you may
never too much regret confiding in me. I need hardly say how
much I feel proud and glad and flattered to see from your letters
and your manner to me that you do think of me and that you do

love me- perhaps even a good deal. I can never understand why it should be so but I hug myself with pleasure that it is so.

I shall be looking forward with great interest to your letter of tomorrow morning (I hope) with a full and true account of what happened at the Kelly's party on Sunday. I am quite sure you will be able to keep your end up with Mrs Duffy. When you put on that consequential air of yours, it requires quite a lot of courage I should say to resist it. In my case anyhow I find it very difficult to resist you at any time but I think the emotion produced is not fear so much as something very different. I always want to take you in my arms and smother you with kisses. By the way talking of kisses I must say that I have formed a very high opinion of the intelligence and good sense of Father Flynn, your recent confessor, and I feel quite grateful to him for making your tender conscience easy on that score. The prospect sounds so promising and <u>appetising</u> that I feel almost inclined to swoop down on you some week and soon and take advantage of the greater generosity which I presume you are now prepared to show me. To tell the honest truth, I'm beginning to feel the want of you more and more every day and <u>worse</u> and <u>worse</u> so that I very much doubt if I shall be able to hang on till Easter without seeing and kissing your dear face again and hearing your dear voice. So don't be surprised if you hear of my arrival in the country about the end of the month. Seriously however, if you wouldn't like me to come- I mean if you think it would be better for me not to come, I will wait and possess my soul in patience until Easter. I'm sure you will all be busy in the next four weeks and I wouldn't like to be keeping you from your work, entertaining a silly love-sick ass like me so I won't speak of it anymore unless you do it beforehand. Glad to hear Christy is improving so much. I suppose Kerrigan was only making a big fellow of himself by making him out to be so bad. Hope everyone at home is well also at Lockardstown I am writing to Mrs S. today. Bad job about Johnnie. Ask him can I help him at all when you see him. Give my regards to everyone. I send you my warmest and sincerest love and kiss your dear hands a thousand times.

your happy husband-to-be
James

Pembroke House
Upper Mount Street
Dublin
14/3/1916

My dearest and best,
    I didn't intend to write to you today but I suppose you would like to have a line so I am taking the opportunity of a few minutes quiet to thank you for today's letter. I haven't a word of news unfortunately to send you. Last night I brought home two or three files of papers from the office to clear up staff matters which have been bothering me for a good while past. Certain of the temporary male clerks at present employed here are likely to be dispensed with about the end of the month and it was up to me to provide an expedient (..) That's one of my particular little worries, to deal with staff questions, rearrange duties for each person, look after the getting of money voted by Parliament for salaries re.(..) and so on and so forth until I get worried to death nearly sometimes and feel inclined to throw a book at the head of some silly ass who comes to me asking what he is to do with some simple case he is dealing with. Well I cleared up the matter fairly well last night, drafted a letter to be sent to the Treasury in the matter and sailed off to bed.

Result sleeplessness for a couple of hours owing to working so late and then I got to thinking about you and how you had enjoyed Mrs Kelly's party and looking forward to your letter this morning. Eventually I went to sleep and dreamed about you, that we had quarrelled- I forget whether before or after marriage- and made it up in the end after a lot of tears and kisses on both sides. I hope the kisses part will come true and that we may miss the quarrel and the tears. I was much amused with your account of Mrs Kelly as a hostess. I told my mother that part of your letter about Ned Casey not being up to the mark for Mrs Kelly and she laughed fit to burst over it. How is it Laddie didn't see the bride? Was he also not up to the mark for the drawing room and was he left to a "carman's treat" in the kitchen!! I'm annoyed that John Duffy should think I wouldn't spend time with him. I never saw him in Hopkin's and am surprised he wouldn't speak himself if he saw me. Was the Mrs with him at the time or was he alone? Sorry to hear Johnnie is still without news. Must close now as there is one of the men at my elbow waiting to see me. I send you my warmest love as usual and wish I could show it in a more practical and satisfying way than on paper.

your devoted lover for ever and ever
James

Togherstown
Ballinea
Mullingar
15th March 1916

My dearest James

I was glad to get your letter this morning I would have written but the evening turned out so bad I could not get it to post I hope you had not been expecting one as I would not like to disappoint my poor hard working man, you should not have worked so late as to take the sleep of yourself- so long as you are working like that you have no need to fast or pray or anything- it takes a lot of obligations off you after. I may go to the post this evening and do the Stations of the Cross. I have gone every evening I could since Lent came in & I always say a little prayer for somebody. You need not be one bit sorry you did not speak to John Duffy- I am very glad you did not let him think someone feels above him.

Mrs S was in Balrath last night. They were telling her there, all John was telling Gertie & Cookie Kiernan the day they paid him a visit. He said the reason I am going to marry you, is because "<u>I am mad he did not marry me- that I was expecting he would</u>" I would not be quite so sore about that as about Jennie- he said she married Corbett because Jim Fay[49] would not marry her and that she wrote scores of letters to him (J Fay), he saw them himself. He told a lot of other stories about other respectable girls all to the effect that they were mad after him & asked him to marry them etc. I think he must be going off his head to say I was thinking of my blood first cousin & a man I always looked on as a mild form of the old boy himself from the few things as I told you, you may form no opinion of him, there was a little foundation for Jennie about the letters, You know J. Fay was really in love with Jennie, & wanted to marry her, he wrote constant to her. She answered a

few of them where she wanted to get him to sell tickets & again
where he said he'd go on a booze the morn he should have a
letter if he had not. I saw the letters she wrote & partly dictated
them; the sarcasm of them I remember well left them as far as
she was concerned that they could be read on the chapel gates-
I know all that rests with you. He speaks of Mother & Mrs S as
Monsheen Fay & Mary Seery- the talk of him in Kelly's could not
be compared to Dan Kiernan's before his bride- enough to make
you happy you did not speak to him if you did see him-
I won't write anymore it has taken me ages to write this, you
would not see by it my hand is shaking. I have a bit of a headache
Bye Bye now dearest James

Tons of warm & bestest love
From your loving
May
I am getting to be a great walker
I never feel my ankle at all

We got currant cake with wine on it & Jenny called it tipsy cake
The hint might suit Nora. She goes in for them

39 Belgrave Square
Rathmines
Dublin
19/3/1916

My dearest May,
You have sent me many letters that I rejoiced at but none
was half so good as your dear letter of this morning. I have been
thinking and wondering about it ever since and the more I think
the more I fail to understand what in God's name ever put a
thought of me in your sweet mind. Recently I have been comfort-
ing myself with the thought that you did like me a good deal but
I never suspected that you had such hidden depths of affection
as the incident of the rose reveals. Good Lord! when I think what
a fellow I am and have been, I feel like the dirt when I imagine it
possible that a prize such as you are could ever love me. I remember the roses you wore that day very well as I remember your
dress and everything you said and did but I have only a very faint
recollection of having picked up the rose for you. Probably I did it

mechanically as an act of politeness without thinking there was
any special significance in it. If you had given me the rose instead
of my restoring it to you, I could have remembered it forever.
The clearest thing I remember about the whole day is that I was
furiously jealous of Ray (the best man) all day especially as you
laughed and joked with him. I remember thinking that it was only
natural you should prefer a man younger and better looking than
me and I half made up my mind there and then to throw up the
prize. That was while we were up the hill. Later on when we were
playing the cards you sat beside me and I plucked up a bit of spirits again but on the whole thinking over the whole day's events
afterwards I was inclined to think my chances were very poor.
One or two little things that happened during my holidays in
August gave me hope, once or twice you allowed your hand to
remain in mine when we shook hands and more especially your
handshake the day I said goodbye that time. I was bursting to
speak to you then but I got no chance and I never had so bad a
heartache as leaving you then, not knowing whether to hope
or despair. All that is over and done with now, thank God, and I
need hardly say how I will cherish your dear sweet gift and mark
of love. You needn't tell me not to do away with it. Do you think
I'm mad to do such a thing? I doubt very much if you will ever get
it back again unless you insist on it. Don't think that is said as a
joke or to flatter you. As I hope for final forgiveness, it is true and I
love and revere my dear and darling all the more if possible when
I know that nearly a year ago she already had regard for me. As
to your being a cool customer as you say, I know very well now
from what you tell me that you are not. I'm glad to hear that you
are thinking of the races. Mrs Seery was asking me would I come
down for them but I said I wasn't sure, not thinking that you
would be likely to go. I hope you will go and maybe you'd think of
inviting me too. I know Mrs S would be only too delighted to give
me lodging for the few days if you wouldn't be too hard-hearted
to refuse to let me come down. Please do let me come down
to see you then. I'm breaking my promise already not to speak
about coming down again until you mentioned it so I won't say
any more now. You know very well what I want and what I long
for every hour and every minute almost. Do you know you are the

last thought at night and the first in the morning? Well it's true anyhow whether you suspect it or not. I have no news at all this time so I will close up with the warmest love and devotion to my dearest girl from her ever faithful and loving
James

National Health Commission (Ireland)
Pembroke House
Upper Mount Street
Dublin
21/3/1916

My dearest and best,
I feel horribly sick with myself because of having disappointed you this morning. I had firmly intended writing you a line yesterday just to show you that I think of you always but I never got as much as a minutes respite yesterday. I came in at ten yesterday (which was very early for me) and never lifted my head till 7 yesterday evening. Imagine I never got as much as a minute for dinner and had to snatch a cup of tea about 4 o'clock to help keep me going. I have had more than a few pretty hard days in this department since I joined it but I can honestly say I never had one a bit worse than yesterday.

Don't think I'm telling you all this mainly in order to "throw flowers at myself" or to enlist your sympathy (though that is always a pleasure to me) but I want to show you that it wasn't my fault that I failed you yesterday. I have been very hard run the last few days. Sunday night I was up till at work. I bought it home on Saturday and of course left it on the long finger till Sunday evening. Last night I went to confession and got rid of a load of trouble with the result that both last night and Sunday night my mind was a bit too active going to bed for sleep with the inevitable result that I got on to the usual topic- yourself- and didn't get to sleep till all hours. However my sleep was very pleasant both nights.

I imagine sometimes that you are watching over me at night and that your prayers and your sweet spirit keep and sustain me. Indeed just to show you that I think it's true I'll let you into a little secret of my confession. The priest in Clarendon Street (you remember we were in it one Sunday together at Mass) told me that he thought there was somebody praying for me. I suppose he was surprised that such a "bad egg" would ever otherwise have the courage to go to confession. So I think you're going to be my guardian angel for I'm sure the poor chap that got that thankless job when I was born has given up on me in despair long ago.

I was delighted to get your letter this morning and especially with the contents. The lock of hair is going with the other treasures. As regards the photo I'm sure I can't imagine who the <u>very plain looking girl</u> with the baby is. I don't think I could have ever seen her anyway. The poor thing will be quite offended if she hears that you have been sending her photo all round the country for strange men to make remarks about her (bow-wow). I'll keep the photo anyhow for a few days and will give it back to you (if you want it) when I see you. Perhaps by that time I will have discovered the identity of the lady!! As regards going down to see you I'd prefer next Saturday to any other because for one thing it would break the miserable wait till Easter more evenly than going later on but if you <u>want</u> to go to the races I could defer it till then or preferably I could go down then also. But if the races are on the 10th or 17th April I'd rather go now. I wouldn't mind deferring my visit till the 3rd April if the races were then but if they are later <u>I want to go now</u>. For one thing I want to see you <u>so much</u> and for another I'm a bit cleaner in spirit than the last time I saw you and could look you in the face and kiss you with less compunction than on my previous visit.

The concert was a huge success as I told you. The Miss O'Connor who played the harp was not one of the O'Connors you met. We must go and hear the harp played some time a good player is performing. She wasn't much so you didn't miss a lot. About Killarney I don't care one way or another and the same as regards the day" Thursday for losses" doesn't bother me. I'd face anything with you by my side, my darling girl, and the only thing I shouldn't like is "no day at all" .Will you let me know in your note about the date of the races and if it is later than the 3rd April please let me come down <u>next</u> Saturday. Will write you again tomorrow. I send you my warmest and dearest love

Your ever loving

James

39 Belgrave Square
Rathmines
Dublin
22/3/1916

My dearest May,

I have started to write this at home on Tuesday at very near midnight and will finish it on Wednesday. The letter I sent you today (Tuesday) was I fear a bit abrupt at the end. Duffy (you remember meeting him here) called in to go to dinner with me and I had to close it up rather hurriedly. If I left it over till the evening I would probably have missed the post. About this watch I am sorry that it is not giving satisfaction. O'Leary in Hopkins told me when I bought it that all watches of the kind are a bit flighty at the start and he asked me to tell you to let him see this watch the next time you were in town in order to have it tested again. I shall call and see him and tell him about it. If you like I could take it back with me when returning to town after my next visit (Saturday next I hope) and I could bring it down to you at Easter. Please yourself though in that respect. As it will be so short now until you are here for good (my good) perhaps you would like to wait till then. I don't see any reason why it shouldn't keep good time all right because it was tested beforehand for three days and was then all right. I'm glad to hear you are so fond of it (I hope for my sake). You will see by my other letter that I am anxious to go down either this week end or next.

If you decide to let come down this week end, I am half inclined to come down on Saturday morning by the 9:15 from Broadstone (11:15 at Castletown) so as to have the day with you. The other train is later and I have to change at Mullingar but perhaps it would be inconvenient for you for me to come on the early train as Saturday is generally a busy day in every house and besides you might be going to Mullingar and might prefer to meet me there and be home with me. I'll leave it all to you as well as the decision whether I come next Saturday or Saturday week. If you say next Saturday let me know by return which trains I am to come on and whether I am to meet you at Mullingar.

It will be delightful to have the details of the marriage to talk over and to be able to settle things once and for all. If you don't care for Killarney it's easy to go somewhere else. I'll make enquiries about other places down south and we can go to one of them and perhaps drop in at Killarney for a day or two on our way home.

I don't mind where I go so long as you go with me. As regards the dress I'm afraid I'm a poor guide as to either colour or make although I could tell you all right whether I liked a dress or not. I was at last Mass on Sunday and we had a passable sermon (quite good for Rathmines) on St Joseph but I'm sorry to say I didn't pass very particular remarks on it. If I had thought of your interest in St Joseph I should have been more attentive.

Judging by the papers, you had a nice row down in Tullamore on Monday night. I suppose you have heard all about it by this. There must be a queer crowd of rowdy element there when such things can happen. I was at another concert last night run by Cope for his choir. Nora is going to him for singing lessons hence

Newspaper review of the concert

my presence at it. I'm sending you the programme in case you might be interested. It was very good all round but nobody we know was performing. Am spun out of news now so will shut up with my warmest love and devotion
   your loving and faithful husband-soon
   James

> Togherstown
> Ballinea
> Mullingar
> 23rd March 1916

My dearest James,
      Many thanks for letter this morn I was glad to get it, I will not bother about watch, you need not either. It may be going alright now; I had no chance of seeing right time since. You had my letter this morn saying to come on Sat. next about the early train, I am afraid I'll have to make the sacrifice until Sat. Evening. Sat is a mass morning & Mother has to go to Mullingar, I might be very busy with extra men & I may not. I can't send wire to say "come I'm idle" but I will meet you in Mullingar if I possible can- I'll make it my business to but don't be disappointed if I don't so now I suppose you won't think a bit the more of me for breaking my promise but it was all your fault like the day of Jennie's wedding. I am sure my letter you had this morning made you laugh. I was very much amused writing such a thing.
I forgot to comment on your letter this morning & others "What day you will let me come etc."- you won't be always that subject to me, do you think will you?- but you might be afraid of me if I

prove very wicked or what they call "a walk over".
At present I have no news, don't forget to bring me the photo of
that girl. Goodbye now dearest James love go leor (is that right?)
From your loving
May
{written on back of letter: " Of course it's on your account I wear
the watch"]

National Health Commission (Ireland)
Pembroke House
Upper Mount Street
Dublin
23/3/1916

  My darling May
      I was overjoyed to get your letter this morning telling me
that I may go down for the weekend to see you. I am writing Mrs
Seery now to ask for lodgings but I don't know yet whether you
will let me go on the early train on Saturday or on the evening
train. When you have decided that point you might please let Mrs
Seery know so that she may know when to expect me. It's really
not a vital matter with me as if I don't go early Saturday I shall
take an extra day instead probably Tuesday as I shall stay Monday in any case but of course naturally the sooner I see you the
sooner I shall be happy.
Until I see you I shall as usual be eating my heart out and one's
heart is very unsatisfying diet. About the photo I'll bring it down
with me. Of course I was only joking about the plain looking girl
as I know very well it is yourself and I could hardly think you plain

Dominic Street, Mullingar

looking since I love you so much! I don't think it's quite fair of you
to try to pretend it is someone else. I haven't shown it around the
house at home so you needn't be afraid on that score. I wrote to
you on Sunday <u>early</u> in reply to your letter enclosing the cher-
ished rose and posted it myself before 4 o'clock long before post
hour so you should have it on Monday. The bould Paddy is to
blame I'm quite sure especially if it bears the Ballinea postmark
4:30 am on Monday.

About Ray and the jealousy I was interested in the account of the
happenings on the hill. I don't blame poor Ray for talking silly.
I'd do it myself only I'm more given perhaps to self-repression. I
don't think you are quite fair in thinking me backward or seem-
ingly indifferent that day. It's a long day since I have been indifferent to you although you're inclined to think I'm only telling
you that to please you. I'm afraid you don't yet understand my
attitude of mind to you for a good while past.

I half suspect Mrs Seery must have guessed how I felt towards
you because whenever your name cropped up she used to mention what age you were and so on. For instance I remember very
well her having told me several times you were not yet 19 and
I remember how I used internally to say "O Lord, put her out of
your head, you d.. fool" I could hardly think anything else when
I considered our relative ages and your extreme youth. For all
these reasons I have always been inclined to stand out of the
running where you were concerned and to give you a fair field
when younger and better men were concerned. For example, I remember somebody remarking last year in connection with Josie
Duffy's marriage that one of the Casey boys might fix a covetous
eye on you at the wedding and I thought to myself that it would
be a shame for me to stand in the way of your happiness if such
came to pass.

Any of the Casey boys that I met would have been a much more
suitable and probably a much better husband for you than I could
ever hope to be. All these considerations restrained me and made
me seem backward. I always wanted you to have the chance of
seeing the merits of the better men and although it would have
cost me many a heartache I'd have been contented to see you
married to somebody else if I was sure you preferred him to your

humble servant, (servant in every sense I hope). I'm afraid I have nothing more to say at the present except that I look forward to seeing you on Saturday.

Be sure to let Mrs Seery know what train to expect me on. From what I have just told you I suppose it is unnecessary to repeat my love or to send you any special loving message now.

I have loved you for many a day, May darling, and I hope we live together in ever increasing love and harmony for a good many years to come. I have no fears <u>now</u> that you will fail in your love and devotion but I distrust myself always.

I kiss my dear girl's sweet face many times and send her my love.

James

Togherstown
Ballinea
Mullingar
24th March 1916

My dearest James

      Were you disappointed today when you got my letter saying not to come until late train but it cannot be helped, you understand I am sure, I can't even say will I meet you in Mullingar or not but I'll meet you some where never fear so don't begin to cry if I'm not at Mullingar when you step out but be a good boy & get the Castlebar train. I guessed you knew the photo but I thought you might doubt when I said that. Glad you did not show it round, be sure to bring it down with you- isn't it a very nice child but I suppose you are not a judge. I think you only guessed it was me- Mrs S did not know me.

Thanks for the compliment "You'd be content to see me married to somebody else" <u>I'll keep that in my nose for you</u>.

I have no news now so good bye with best & fondest love
from your loving
May

Again on the 25th James came to visit at Togherstown and there's a short break in the letter writing

Togherstown
Ballinea
Mullingar
29^(th) March 1916

My dearest James,

How did you get back last night? I hope I will have a letter in the morning saying how you got on. Were you lonely etc. I was not so lonely as I was the last time you left but I miss you very much today. I feel inclined to be expecting you every minute but your (sic) not coming. It would scarcely do for you to step out & say "you were going to see May"

Mrs Seery saw Father Moran in the train as it shunted back last night that is why we waited thinking the train might stop & we could tell you I am sure you would have liked the company as well as the chat with your cousin. I am going up to the stations now & will post this to you I have not a word of news so I hope you will excuse this short letter. How did you find your Mother & Nora? I hope they did not think you looking the worse of your visit. I hope your Mother is good heart with the thought of becoming so soon a mother-in-law.

Good bye now dearest James fondest best & warmest love from your loving

May

National Health Commission (Ireland)
Pembroke House
Upper Mount Street
Dublin
29/3/1916

My dearest May,

I got back all right last night very glad to see the fire after a very cold and not particularly cheery journey. There were very few people in the train so that we ran through without a stop from Enfield. That was about the only comfort in an otherwise depressing journey. I found everybody very well and looking out for the news but I'm afraid I'm a bad hand at news.

My mother was anxious to know if we had definitely fixed <u>the day</u> but I had to disappoint her in that also. I wish you'd try and induce your mother to fix it for the 1st June. That's the day I'm looking forward to and I shall feel awfully disappointed if the marriage doesn't take place then. I must start to make preparations for it now. There's a good deal in the way of painting and papering that I should like to see done and I must try and induce my landlord to do the house up generally for your reception. Of course I must have it looking its best when my dear bride comes home to it. When a man gets a pearl (that's what Ray called you wasn't it?) he must get a proper setting for it. I must at any rate have <u>our</u> bedroom done up and I had it in mind before going down to ask you about it but forgot to somehow. My mother was suggesting that you should use the small room in front of the drawing room and that I should get a large wardrobe made for it that would hold your clothes. The one in <u>our</u> room is small enough for my own clothes at present and would be quite unsuitable for you. We can talk it over when you come up at Easter and of course whatever you decide on can be arranged. It will be an extra pleasure in making my own arrangements to have the additional job of fixing a nest for you.

I hope you weren't lonely last night. I haven't yet had the time to get lonely although I feel the loss of you every moment but I suppose I'll be as restless and dissatisfied as ever after another day or so.

I'm writing this under forced draught as I have a lot of things waiting over for my return so I hope you won't mind if I don't send you a long letter there is a conference of various of the various Insurance Commissioners England Ireland and Scotland in London next week and I shall have a lively time till it is over. I was talking to Mr Gallagher[50], my chief, today and he suggested my coming with him quite as I expected. Of course I cried off at once but he may return to the charge again.

How would you like your poor little man running the risk of submarines and Zeppelins eh? Will write to you again tomorrow, perhaps a longer and more satisfactory letter. This is a very poor, unloving kind of letter I think but I know you know me well enough now and what my feelings towards you are. Remember to all. I send you my dearest and fondest love

    Your loving
    James

Togherstown
Ballinea
Mullingar
30ᵗʰ March 1916

My dearest James
Your letter this morning was indeed very welcome you
were very good to write I don't know what I'll do if my poor man
is brought off to London I hope you won't any way I'll be very
anxious about you until you will be landed safe home again but
perhaps you won't be obliged to go yet.
Yes! I think we may decide on the first of June- it was not my
mother it was myself was putting off deciding because I was
afraid of having to change the day it is so unlucky I hear. You are
a darling man to be planning improvements on the house for me
I will never half appreciate your goodness the only reward I ever
can offer you is my few very poor indeed prayers, nothing else- it
is not my heart is stopping me, there are a hundred things I would
like to do if only I had half the goodness in me, but alas I have
nothing at all but my youth and the wish for all the other neces-
saries to enter on married life.
I did not think on any of my dress points yet the white silk I know
would be very nice but when I think of poor Jennie so far away I
know she would love to see me married but I think it would make
her extra lonely if she heard of me in white silk she would like to
pluck me when I have it on & make me look well I dread for that
reason to have any little fuss- she is such a child (the old woman
talking)
I commenced to feel & see those things so many years ago that it
is no wonder I feel such an ancient piece of goods, and if I guess
rightly it is one of the things old people dislike in the young is being what they call "an ould fashioned lassie" I am sure you often
heard it said.
Mrs Seery has just called, she told me thank you for enquiring so
soon about Johnnie he had a letter to day ~~about~~ from Meagher
who gave him very good hopes he will get the job any way the
poor thing ought to be old sick of country charms.
I have not a bit of news so I will say a fond & loving bye to my

Wedding of Jenny Fay and Jack Corbett 1915, the bride wore white silk

dearest man
From his loving girl
May
I dreamt last night I was getting married not to you but I had you as a guest you might be the better off man too.
I'm off to the post with this.

National Health Commission (Ireland)
Pembroke House
Upper Mount Street
Dublin
30th March 1916

    My darling May,
    I have had a divil of a rush today and haven't been able to write to you until now (6pm) so that I shall have to pay a late fee of ½ d if I'm to catch the night's post. So now ain't I good when I think you worth a ½ d extra. You had my letter this morning I hope telling you that I got home all right. I found my cousin, Baby Finn[51], before me, she was up for a week. It never rains but

it pours so we had a letter yesterday from Mag Moran[52] to say
that "me uncle frank" was coming up to the Doctor so we shall
have him also for goodness knows how long. He arrived yesterday evening. He is nearly stone deaf and naturally the pleasure of
talking to him is not very great so between all we won't be sorry
when we bid goodbye to him. Tell Mrs Seery that he arrived yesterday and I'm sure she will understand how pleased my mother
is over his visit. I don't think I'm naturally inhospitable but he is
such a nuisance at home that they naturally encourage him to
stay away when he comes up to us and the result usually is that
his visit tends to become a visitation. However that's another of
life's little worries and I needn't trouble you with it any more. I'm
sorry I missed seeing Frank Moran in the train. I was out at Mullingar for a paper but I didn't see any sign of him there either and
I didn't look out at Killucan when I suppose he alighted. Passing
back through Castletown Station I saw you both but imagined
you didn't see me. Have you thought of the races since? If you do
will you let me know in time as I'm half inclined to go since it will
be my last appearance as a free man. Isn't that a serious matter
to think on that my freedom is over and done with in another
four weeks. I'm beginning to feel quite melancholy at the prospect.
I hope you won't feel worried over my mentioning that I might
be going to London. There is not the least chance of my going
this time as I have definitely refused to go with the Accountant
and I know well he will not press the matter further. I was only
joking when I mentioned it to so you needn't think you are going to get rid of me so easy as you imagined. I'm glad to know
from your letter that you have been feeling lonely for me as it
shows that you are beginning to feel that I am necessary for you
just as you, my love, are necessary for me. I know very well now
that I couldn't get on without you any longer and that I certainly
couldn't live a good and proper life without you. If anything
happened now to separate us I know that life would have no
further joy or interest for me. It wasn't at all in a joke that I said
to you some time ago that you would have to be my guardian
angel for the future. I do really and truly mean it and the more I
get to know you and understand the truth and goodness in you

the more I realise what an unhoped-for and undeserved blessing from God I received when I won your love.

I have no news at all so will conclude with fondest and warmest love to my dearest and best girl

From your own loving
James

Jane "Baby" Finn

Togherstown
Ballinea
Mullingar
31ˢᵗ March 1916

My dear James
Many thanks for letter of today I was very glad you thought me worth ½d stamp & better still worth the trouble of it you are very good any way to write so constant but I must put in for my share of praise- the boys are in Mrs Seery's to day & for the past few days sowing spuds & if I did not go to the post myself I am afraid you would miss many a letter (and you would miss a lot) I was delighted to hear you have not to go to London I wonder you cannot refuse like that.

I hope you will enjoy your uncle Frank's visit & that his hearing will improve- is that what he is being treated for the poor thing- he will miss a lot of trouble too, I know I often wished I couldn't hear- it would have spared me many a sore heart.

About the races I don't know how will I go but that might not prevent you from going. I will leave it to you to decide will I go to the races or go to be with you in Dublin for a weekend we will be busy from this out but as far as Mother is concerned she is already weaning herself of me & would be quiet (sic) willing to see go about but that is no reason I would leave her in the lurch as they say until must I suppose the earliest that happy must leave can be is the first of June. Besides I wonder would everyone think it proper for me to go alone to your house. Of course you will be down for Easter Mrs S says you intend coming Holy Thursday & I suppose stay the week, will you? I am already looking forward to that visit we can celebrate the festival in fine style Johnnie C is in great humour over the letter he got yesterday. I have no other news now I hope I will get to post this easily

Very best love & good wishes from your loving
May

National Health Commission (Ireland)
Pembroke House
Upper Mount Street
Dublin
31st March 1916

My dearest May,

Thanks very much for your loving letter to-day which has brightened the whole day for me. I am glad that you are thinking of the 1st June as the settled date even although you haven't made up your mind finally on the point. Personally I think it's all tommy rot about bad luck and so on if the date is deferred or if the day is wet or if you're married in May and so on. A great deal of the luck depends on people themselves and although I don't deserve anything in that way I am hoping that I may dodge the bad luck under your tender and sheltering wing.

I hardly imagine that you will have the bad luck anyhow for you don't deserve it so I ought to be quite safe as long as I hang on to your petticoat. So far as I'm concerned I'm prepared to chance my arm if you made up your mind to go off immediately after Easter and I'm leaving all decisions of that nature to you, especially now that I know you're such an "ancient piece of goods" and such an" ould granny". So I'll hug the prospect of the 1st of June to my heart and keep my love hot and my heart up with the hope of my dream coming true. I hope your dream anyhow won't come true. I'm very, very fond of you right enough but I doubt if I could endure being a guest at your wedding to somebody else, however much I might wish you luck and happiness. I expect you must have been thinking about what I told you when I was down and dreamt about it. About the white silk I do hope you will decide on it. I'd love to see my darling girl in white silk for I'm sure she would look glorious in it. I'm afraid though if you looked

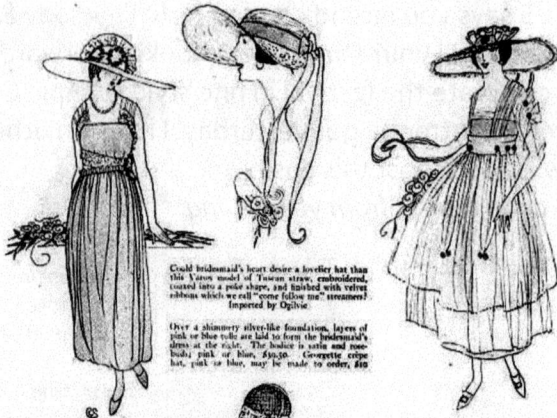

too well on the morning of our marriage that I'd be nearly afraid to touch you and then what would I do? Jennie wouldn't be vexed at you for liking to look your best on the most important day of your life, indeed she'd probably be more vexed at the thought you had put the idea of white silk out of your head on her account. In any case you can bring it with you on your honeymoon and put it on for her and she can pluck you to pieces for all I care. I'll be <u>tired</u> of you by then!

I hope you will continue to remember me in your prayers as I want them all very badly indeed. I'm trying to pull myself together so as to be a little better worthy of you and the struggle is a hard one. I doubt sometimes whether I'll ever be any use to you or anyone else and upon my word the more I think of it the more I realise what a very unwise and innocent girl you are ever to agree to chance yourself with this miserable son of a gun. Talking about guns, the Volunteers held a big meeting in town last night to protest against the deportations of Volunteers organisers and

there was a row afterwards with the police in which revolvers were freely used. No one luckily was hurt but there were a lot of shots fired passing the Recruiting office in Grafton Street. I don't know what is going to be the end of it all but I hope for the best. No other news here I think. Mrs Ross of Longford was up seeing us yesterday evening and I believe there was something between the brother James Fitzpatrick and Miss Dooner of Longford but it's all off now she tells me. Mother and everyone here well as usual. Give my regards to your mother and all and with my warmest and fondest love and kisses to yourself
Always your loving
James

Togherstown
Ballinea
Mullingar
1ˢᵗ April 1916

My dearest James

I was glad to get your nice letter this morn I got it quite early too – and it's a lovely day the nicest we have had for a long while. I would love to be married on a day like this. It would suit the white silk alright- I can't really know what to say about the white silk until I see what they have in Keelans[53] where I intend getting my dress. I know very well Jennie would not wish for anythink to be the means of putting me off getting what dress I preferred, neither did she ever say anything to make me think what I said- in fact she never mentioned the like even once, but I got that notion that it would be bad taste, still if I can possibly clear my brain of all the obsticles (sic) I will get the white silk when you like it or rather when you think you do because you don't know but it may look awkward on me & it might be quiet possible if I did look very awkward you would be tired of me before the honeymoon was finished. It's worse in my eye to look awkward looking than bad looking I am after saying more in connection with the white silk than it's worth, anyway I don't intend to worry about my dress & its effects at least its effects I will leave to providence- it has done a lot for me without even asking, when it won your admiration or what would I call it sympathy! It's horrid to think of the Volunteers & those rows I hope all that will be over before I get to settle down in Dublin

Did anyone make any April fool of you to day or since I made the January fool of you pretending I was everything good etc. But I cannot throw it at you yet for another few months when I shout like the lads "June fool!" "June fool!"

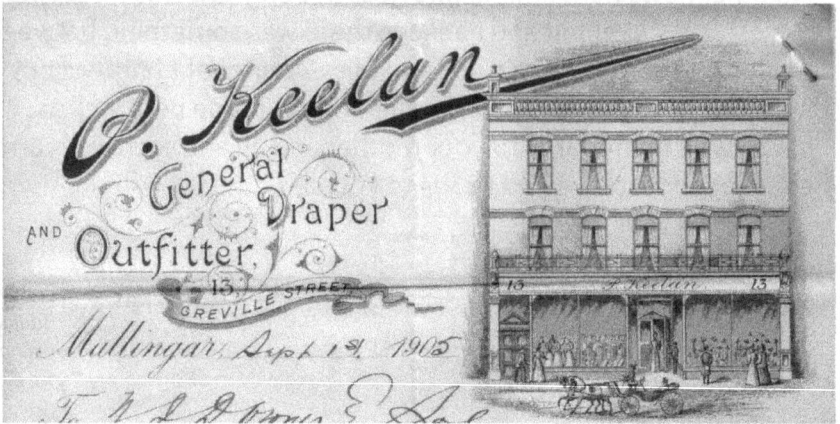

Keelans Draper, Mullingar

Whoes (sic) fault was it that "the Misses Dooner case" did not go any better I wonder
I have not a word of news so I will conclude with very best & warmest love to my dearest James
From your loving
May
I am already thinking of your Sunday letter Second Mass

39 Belgrave Square
Rathmines
Dublin
1st April 1916

My dearest darling May,
I hadn't the least expectation of getting a letter from you and so I was all the more delighted to have it. I guessed the last few days that you probably had to do your own post and for that reason I didn't think you'd write yesterday. I know very well it is awfully good of you to write to me so often and I had it on the tip of my pen to say so yesterday but I was interrupted as I am very frequently and forgot it afterwards. About the race if it is a choice

for me between seeing you at the races and seeing you in town I
prefer the latter of course but I was hoping that I might have both
pleasures. If however I can only have one of the two, I plump for
you coming up for a few days rather than seeing you for an hour
or two in a crowd at Mullingar.

I have been talking the matter over with my mother and she will
leave it to yourself when you come up. Nora and Moll will probably be going away this day week for about three weeks and
will be back shortly after Easter and perhaps you would like to
have either of them here at the time. They would be useful to
you if you were buying things or anything of that sort and besides you will probably get tired of my dull company after a while
and might like for a change to have someone younger than my
mother to speak to. It will be an awful disappointment to me not
to be able to see you until Easter if you decide not to come up
before then but I suppose it can't be helped. I hope your mother
won't be vexed at me for dragging you away from home during
the spring hurry. I'm sure you'll all be very busy now for the next
couple of months for things look now as if the spring was at last
starting in earnest.

The last few days have been perfect here and today is like a
Summer day. Hadn't I the devil's own luck not to go down this
weekend instead of last. It would have been so pleasant to be
rambling about with my own dear girl, but I can't complain even
so for I had her all to myself in the house if I couldn't go outside
and what more could I want. In any case I expect to have a lovely
time at Easter when I shall probably be free for at least a week
and of course I'm burning for it to be here now. I hope you will be
extra sweet and nice and good to me then and if you do I'll bring
you an extra large Easter egg so now be a "dood ittle dirl" and
you'll see what you'll get. I'm afraid I have no pleasant news of
any sort to tell you. My chief, Gallagher, is going off to London on
Monday morning and although he pressed me again to accom-
pany him I declined so your poor little man is safe for the present. I don't envy him his job especially as they have had another
Zeppelin raid in England and in any case he will have a lot of very
troublesome and exacting work to get through which I know very
well without blowing horns that I could handle better myself as I

am much more familiar with the particular job being dealt with. I don't expect a letter tomorrow so I hope, love, that you won't give yourself the fag of tramping up to Loughnavalley for me. It is dear and good of you but I hope you won't be putting yourself about on my account. You must be getting to be a great walker when you can do that walk every day without being tired. How is the poor ankle getting on? I suppose well or you wouldn't be able to walk so well. Give my love to all and with fondest and most enduring love to my dearest and best girl

Always your loving & devoted
James

39 Belgrave Square
Rathmines
Dublin
April 2nd 1916

My dearest love

You are awfully good to write to me so constantly and especially when you have to do all your own messages. Your letters make me very happy so that I don't feel the day pass until I am hearing from you again. All the same I'm not so selfish as to wish you to write to me <u>every</u> day so please don't be putting yourself about writing except when you find it convenient. I was out walking for a good while today but my company was not so pleasant as I could have had if I had only deferred my country visit until this Sunday. I was thinking of you all the time and wondering what you were doing but I suppose you were busy with house work at the time and had no time to spare for such a worthless chap as me. The weather these days makes you long for holidays and to be able to get away from the treadmill of the office especially when you know what pleasure and happiness await you if you could only manage to get the liberty. However it's not long now till Easter next Thursday fortnight and it won't be long passing and six weeks after that will be the day of days. I'll start marking them off day by day from now on like I used to do at school and I'll keep my heart warm and my hopes up in the meantime. I'm sure I'll have a lovely time at Easter and on the whole I'm not sorry that you are not anxious to get to the races. I'd be bound to go down to them, nothing could keep me away and as I couldn't for shame's sake spend another weekend in Lockardstown so soon I'd only see you for a few minutes in a crowd and it would only increase my heartache rather than relieve it. It will be much better to have you up for a while than that and I feel like hugging you now (I wish I could!!) for being such a dear good little girl as to agree to come up. My mother will be delighted to have you for as long as you'll stay, sure it's hardly worth your while going back and your own little man will worship you and the ground you stand on all the time.

By the way when I come down at Easter I'd like to buy you something just to show my love. Would you like anything special? How about a scarf or gloves or something of that sort? If you wish it, I could get Nora to help me buy and so you could be sure of the taste being all right, if I bought myself I'd probably make an awful mess of it. Nobody made an April fool of me, I wish I had been with you for the pleasure of having it done to me but I know the June fooling will be the best and sweetest in the world. You're quite right in saying that you made a January fool of me or perhaps hardly a <u>January</u> one because it was a very long time before January that you turned my silly head. You have a lot to answer for in that way so I hope you will do your full and proper wifely duty when you pledge yourself.

Indeed I know very well you will but I like to joke you about it in any case, and I like to talk about it or think about it when I'm alone. No news at all today except the lovely weather. The boys must be killed these days with the rush of the spring work so long deferred. Hope they're sowing plenty of spuds and oats because we might all have to live on them this year. Give my regards to your mother, Nano and all and my heart's dearest and warmest love for my darling
From her loving
James

National Health Insurance Commission (Ireland)
Pembroke House
Upper Mount Street
Dublin
3rd April 1916

My dearest May,
I have a minute or two to spare so I think I had better send you a note. It will have to be a short one however so you must be

satisfied with it just as it is. In replying to your letter of yesterday I should probably have told you that I was joking when I said in a previous letter that I'd be tired of you before the honeymoon was over. You know very well that is not true and I hope in God it never will come true. I'd rather a thousand times die than that the time should ever come when I should so cruelly wound the tender and affectionate heart of my dearest and best girl as to ever waver for a moment in my love and respect for you. I have often told you that I have a very poor opinion indeed of myself- I have very good reason for it because I know myself better than you or anyone else does- and for that reason I always fear and distrust myself and think that perhaps a day would come when – the grace of God failing me- I might be unkind or neglectful of you. I pray heaven that I may die first.

Today is a bit of a change from the days just past. It's a bit cloudy and inclined to turn chilly again and would not I fear be quite suitable for white silk. I hope that we will have the luck of good weather for our little celebration and for the honeymoon too. I think it would be no harm if you started praying for it. The sooner you get your petition in the better for perhaps someone else might be praying for rain that day and it would be rotten luck to have a wet day for ones wedding never to speak of having a wet honeymoon which would "put the lid on it". Accountant sailed off for London this morning, I believe, without me thank goodness. There have been three separate and distinct Zeppelin raids on

James' cousin, Jim Finn

the east coast of England in the last three nights[54], Friday Saturday and Sunday and I expect the death toll and the injuries will be tremendous. I expect people in England are getting very frightened over the whole business. We had Jim Finn round last night and he was telling me that he is on the mail boat work for the last few days and expects to have a few trips this week also. I don't envy him his job although I must say that if I had to cross at present it would hardly cost me a thought. Perhaps I'm a bit of a fatal-

ist in these matters or perhaps it is that I think that if the good
Lord wants to hit you, He can do it as handy in your bed as on the
"ocean wave".

 Let me know about the Easter present. I mean to get you something whether you like it or not so you might as well let me know
what you would prefer as to have me spending money on something that perhaps wouldn't please you. Am spun out now both
in time and news so I will close with my heart's warmest and (I
hope) enduring love to the best and sweetest and dearest and
truest little girl in the world.

Always your loving
James

4th *April, 1916*

My dearest May,

  I was <u>awfully</u> disappointed today at not getting a line from
you and now I am inclined to be alarmed for fear you are knocked
up or anything of that sort. I hope that is not the case and that I
may have a line from my dearest girl tomorrow to say that she is
all right. Will you <u>please</u> write me a line by return if you haven't
already done so to say if there is anything up.

I have no news at all today, there is some considerable excitement and talk in the office today (and I suppose in all Dublin Government offices) over an increase in the daily attendance of the
clerical staff in all Government Departments from 7 to 8 hours.
It doesn't affect me personally very much because I have never
been able since I came here to get away at the normal hour of de-
parture (4:45pm) but while I have done that voluntarily all right,
I don't feel obliged to the authorities (the British Government in
this case) for increasing my attendance compulsorily by an extra
hour. I don't however intend to come in any earlier in the morning than I do at present and as you know that is not very early.
So they can take it or leave it at that. In the case of the rank and
file however it is a real hardship and I expect there will be a good
deal of soreness, but their resentment or protests are not in any
case likely to do them any good, because the great British Public
whom they would have to appeal to (the Irish Public don't count
in these days of small nationalities) think that all Civil Servants
have nothing to do and are paid handsomely for doing it.

I have no other news. In connection with the Tullamore affair I
hear that the local recruiting sergeant organised the mob that as-
saulted the Volunteers and paid a lot of them half a crown apiece
for the job. This is from the horse's mouth and will be proved up
to the hilt at the inquiry. Regards to all and warmest love and
kisses to my dear girl
Your loving
James

National Health Insurance Commission (Ireland)
Pembroke House
Upper Mount Street
Dublin
5th April 1916
{Wed}

My darling May,
        I have several things to say to you today and I am afraid I
haven't much time but I'll try to get everything off my chest. First
I was delighted to get your letter. I have had my tongue hang-
ing out for the last couple of days looking out for a line from you
and my heart has been down in my boots every morning when
I got a disappointment. I am grieved that my poor darling has
been knocked up I was just thinking as much when I didn't hear
yesterday but I hope sincerely that you are on the mend now.
About coming up to town I'm <u>awfully</u> disappointed that you
won't come. Of course I know very well when our marriage was
coming off and how near Easter was to it but I don't see why that
should stop you. As regards people saying that I was backing
out, I had the idea that perhaps you would come back with <u>me</u>
at Easter and I don't see how, if you could be induced to do that,
how the peoples tongues could wag but perhaps coming back in
my company would be a highly improper and outrageous thing
to do. I'm afraid I'm not very clear on nice points of good conduct
and morals such as that.
As to the races I must go now since you have made up your
mind to go but I certainly don't feel inclined to spend the money
merely for the fleeting pleasure of a look at you in a crowd so I
think I'll brazen it out with Mrs Seery and come down on Saturday evening next <u>unless you forbid me.</u> I'm writing to her now to
feel my way and if she gives me any encouragement I feel more

than inclined to go and chance your displeasure. I'm more than
half ashamed to trouble her though and I'm afraid both you and
your mother and herself will think I'm mad. Praps I am I should
not wonder indeed if I were when I think soberly of the luck I have
had. Now I want you like a darling to write me a line by return
(I'll have it on Friday) to say whether you would be very much
displeased if I came down for the week end and go to the races
with you rather than go down straight on Monday to Mullingar.
I'd simply hate to see you at the races and not be able to steal a
kiss or get a word in private with you without people looking on
and criticising. So will you please let me come down, love. I'll get
Nora to help me buy something nice in the way of a glove but <u>let
me know your size by Friday</u> so that I can bring them with me. I
have very little news since I wrote to you yesterday you anything
I knew. The Accountant will not be back till Monday probably but
he will be in time to take over things for me. You mustn't worry
on that score. I can always manage a day or two that way when
I want. Remember me to all and tell your mother not to be too
hard on me for coming down so soon but I can't help it. Warmest
and most enduring love for my dearest and best
From your loving
James

Togherstown
Ballinea
Mullingar
6th April 1916

My dearest James
I was glad to get your letter this morn even tho' you were
not in the best of spirits or humour with my changing my mind
& being so long about making it up but I have this much settled
I won't go to town at Easter so I suppose you had better chase
down for the week and Mrs Seery says you are very welcome
of course for my part you know know well what a comfort your
presence will be more than your letter We can have a good talk
when you do come The post man is waiting
The boys are delighted they had great fair
Very best love now my dear James from your loving girl
May
Excuse haste please About glove I'm not really sure the size that

fits me I think it ought to be 6 or 5 1/2 I nearly always guess by looking at them your very very loving May

My darling May

I got back safe & sound and found all right. Moll had only gone down yesterday to the country to Mrs Shiel[55] so I expect Mrs Seery won't have either herself or Nora before tomorrow. I hope they will turn up anyhow and not disappoint her after her making preparations for them. My mother had a painting con-tractor in with her on Monday about the papering of the house so it will start immediately after Easter. It will be a most horrible

job but I suppose it can't be helped. The house is very dirty and in need of doing up at present but I hope it will look nice after the job is done. Was Mrs Seery making any remark since about Louis[56] or was she vexed that I had heard the news in your house. I hope I didn't put my foot in it too badly by my long tongue yester-day evening.

Today is very windy but a lovely warm day so far and very pleas-ant to be out. Tell Mrs S. I might as well have stayed over for another day. Punchestown is on for two days you know and we always get an office holiday for the races, half the staff going one day and the other half on the second day. Result is that both yesterday and today things were very quiet and so far as wish is concerned I might as well be off. In one way how-ever it is just as well I came back as the Accountant is away today and I am in consequence monarch of all I survey and it would be

exceedingly awkward if we were both away together. I must peg into the work like the deuce for the next week until Easter as I have a large mountain of work to get into ship shape before June. Our auditors will be down on us for their usual half yearly check at the end of May just when I'm away so I must have everything in apple-pie order for them. This will be the first time I have ever been away during their visit and the Accountant is full of forebodings that things will not go well but I feel sure the others will be quite capable of handling the situation. Am quite stumped for news today so will conclude. Tell Mrs Seery that we have me Uncle Frank for another week. I must try and make up my mind about the best man before Easter. Warmest and most heartfelt love to my dearest and best,
     From your loving, James

                                                      Togherstown
                                                        Ballinea
                                                       Mullingar
                                                  12th April 1916

     My dearest James
          How are you are after your very expensive trip I hope you got back safely I want to take Jocie Casey's advice & not loose (sic) you too simply but I dare say you have become so much accustomed to the journey up & down now there is no fear of you being lost or even tired. How did you find your mother- lonely I am sure not having Nora there. She must have felt it you to go & leave her alone & of course someone else would feel it if you stayed so God help my poor man he is really "between the Devil & the dark blue sea". Like myself I suppose you looking forward to Easter but you have not long to wait when I see it coming so near I feel ashamed of myself to have let you come so often during the Holy Season I don't know what to say to seeing you Holy week I know I won't see you Good Friday anyway for <u>sure</u> & for <u>certain</u>.
Did your Mother inquire if you had decided on your best man I wonder will Mrs S. be jealous I had given her a hint of your intentions to have some of her boys and she was quiet pleased- Oh by the way she got out of the bag about Louis. Mrs S. told him not on any account to tell Tommy – he told him in a terrible secret &

Tom told C.- in another awful secret so that's the way the awful secrets go. What harm when it comes off it will be all over. I am going down now to meet Nora & Moll they will have a nice drive this evening if they have a middling nag but it would be a bit chilly if they were slow.

My Mother is praising the snapshots of the Castle to Jennie, said Jack had an artistic eye Jennie told Jack of course & "he said he had a more artistic eye than James Finn" has he, he did not mean as far as snapshots goes you know. We had a letter from her to-day she forgot to mention in yesterday's that she liked to the idea of the white satin for me & to have it very full & I will look really Loidy looking she said. Do you know Jennie admires my appearance in general more than Nano's although she knows Nano is the best looking but good looks are very little after all although they are supposed to be better fortune in girls.

I have not a word of news now so I will say goodbye with my very best love to my dearest man

    Your loving May

Jack Corbett was a photography enthusiast, he made this triple exposure photograph of Jenny

Nano Fay, the youngest, she never married

13ᵗʰ April 1916

My dearest May,

I was delighted to have your letter this morning not that you had
very much news in it but I was glad to get it as showing that you
had been thinking of me yesterday. I was telling the news about
Louis at home and my mother was of course delighted to hear
that he is getting fixed up at last. It seems to be quite the rage at
present to get married. I had a letter from George Clitheroe last
night from England to say that he is going off next with Miss Wil-
lette, I suppose some English girl. I don't know whether you ever
met him but Mrs Seery did and she will be interested to hear that
he also as well as myself is losing the "freedom of the city" so
soon. He is at present on night work, he tells me, from 8 at night
till 9 next morning and won't be able to get off even for a day for
his wedding so he is earning his bit as well as doing it for his country. I am afraid you were all disappointed yesterday about Nora &
Moll turning up as promised. Moll only went down to the country
on Tuesday evening, goodness knows what kept her till then, and
of course she wouldn't have been able to get out of Mrs Shiel on
Wednesday and after that I suppose she had to go to Lissavra⁵⁷
to Moran's for a few hours anyhow. I hope they both turned up
today for I know very well if they disappoint that Mrs Seery will
be very mad over it. About Easter of course I'm looking forward
to it already and of course I must see you on Good Friday as well
as every other day whether you like it or not.
You'll have to be promising to love honour and <u>obey</u> in a month
or so now so you might as well be starting to get accustomed
to it. Anyhow as regards Good Friday I promise to be very good
and not to annoy you but I <u>must</u> see you. I'll go round the stations with you or anything you like that way but I <u>will not</u> be put
on the solitary confinement punishment. I was amused to hear
that Corbett thinks he has better taste than I have. I suppose it is
always invidious to make comparisons and besides I should like to
live on good terms with my sisters-in-law but I must say that I'm
quite satisfied that I got the pick of the bunch. We talked over the
question of the best man yesterday evening and I'm afraid I can't

get over Pat Moran[58]. I will break the news to Mrs Seery when I
go down and I hope she will take it all right. Anyhow I can't please
everyone and I suppose someone is bound to be vexed. We hear
today that the eight hour day in the Civil Service is knocked on
the head so that is so much to the good.
No other news. I send you my warmest and most heartfelt love
   From your loving James

                                                    14ᵗʰApril 1916
   My dearest May,
      I haven't time to write hardly today but I don't like to let
you think that I have been forgetting you so this is to show you
that I don't. My mother had a line from Nora this morning from
Lockardstown. We were glad to see by it that the two girls did not
give Mrs Seery a complete disappointment but I suppose they did
not turn up as soon as she expected them. They are both returning this evening I believe so I expect to have a lot of news when I
get home. I have been up to the neck in work since I came back
and have hardly time to bless myself (even if I wanted to) from
the time I come in in the morning till I go away in the evening. I
forgot whether I told you in my letter yesterday that the eight
hour day has been knocked on the head so that is one small comfort although it is really very little relief one way or another to
me. I have to get through the load some way or another whether
it takes seven hours a day or no. I have really no news at all and
besides I must catch the post which leaves in about 20 minutes so
will you please excuse me.
I send you my warmest love and kisses (in spite of the heat)
   Your loving, James

                                                    Togherstown
                                                    Ballinea
                                                    Mullingar
                                                    14ᵗʰApril 1916

   My dearest James
      I was very glad to get your letter this morning I hope you
were not looking out for one from me as I could not manage to
post, we had Nora & Josephine to tea. Moll did not come to Mrs
Seery's at all but will meet Nora in Castletown this evening &
they both start together. Nano and I are going to the station for

the drive. I hope they will have good weather it is not very pleasant these days, the shows of hail would almost cut through you
We were in Mrs Seery's yesterday & met Mag Moran there, were
asked to tea whatever time they came, having 12 o'clock dinner,
we were anxious for an early tea & we took it at home thinking
we would not get in at Mrs S until all hours so she met us at the
door with a very sharp salute & repeated it several times so that
it made the night I might say <u>unpleasant</u> I can't always look over
that cutting way as a joak. I hope Mrs S will look over <u>not being
best man</u>
I did not settle in my own mind yet how I'll see you on Good
Friday- it would be the dear stations I do with you by my side- unless I get a very much stronger will I will give up all prayers after
June I never can pray when I'm near you- as far as the love honour
& obey goes, I intend to commence in true & take up the poker &
say I'll be the boss, that reminds me of a very funny dream I had,
of a very lengthy dispute with you where I wanted to buy some-
thing <u>very necessary</u>, <u>if it is necessary</u> I can't say what it is (don't
think it is something belonging to a bedroom, it is not!) but I was
very determined on getting it & failed, but in a very bad state of
mind. Mrs S said no more about Louis he is going down Sunday
next to settle all, you will say there is no news in this letter either
but I have none I did not meet <u>Clitheroe,</u> he wasn't a catholic was
he?
> Good bye my dearest & best James
> With all my love
> Your own girl
> May

15th April, 1916

My dearest love,

I was delighted to get your letter today but you needn't
have apologised for not writing on Thursday. I hadn't the least
hope of a letter yesterday morning so I wasn't disappointed
(blessed are they that expect nothing)as I knew very well that the
chances were very much against your being able either to write
or to post even if you could write.

I'm sorry to hear that Mrs Seery was nasty to my little girl the other evening. I'm sure she was a bit worrying all right and I know very well that her jokes cut pretty deeply at times if you mind her but I hope you won't pay too much attention to what she says as her bark is always worse than her bite. I must face her whatever happens when I go down about the best man as I can't put it off any longer. I hope she will take it reasonable anyway.

I was sorry to see that you take me so seriously to heart although of course it flatters me very much. I thought I had enough on my conscience when I diddled you into agreeing to marry me but if I have in addition the load on my conscience of making you give up all your prayers and other good works I don't know what will become of me. I hope it won't be quite so bad as that and that you will be content to go and do the stations with me on Good Friday and be good and loving and sweet afterwards as you always otherwise are. Sometimes I don't know when you talk that way whether you are joking or not or whether you really do scruple being fond of me or kissing me with the freedom and frankness which is only reasonable in the case of us two.

I don't see what harm you do even if you did think of me and love me on Good Friday as well as on any other day. So far as I am concerned my conscience is not only quite clear in loving and thinking about you but I know and am convinced as I never was of anything before that my only hope of salvation lies in loving you and thinking of you always.

I am always a better and a cleaner man when I think of you and I intend to cling to that last straw like the drowning man. In view of what I say, I imagine it will be easy enough for you to boss me even without the poker but I hope you will not be too severe although I'd certainly advise you to be firm. Moll & Nora got back alright but they didn't have much news for us. Things here are very quiet and nothing at all interesting happening. Give my regards to all and with my warmest and deepest love to my dear and darling

Always your loving & devoted
James

Togherstown
16th April 1916

My dearest James
    I got your letter yesterday & today you were very good to write I have only a minute to write. Laddy is going to Loughnavally besides I have no news only that Louis was down seeing his girl & all is settled Louis is out & delighted with her thinks she is the best of them etc. Johnnie has heard nothing since he is gone to Mullingar today with the Dr & Tommy the latter is gone to bury John Allen[59] with whose people he has great sympathy.
Last night Mrs S called for Mother & both went to see Fr Donellan he does not seem to have got out of his trouble very much yet his sleep is still effected (sic) it seems to have gone very hard on him he was glad to see them I hope Mrs S will take P. Moran as best man in good parts. I am pitying Nora & Moll if they have weather anything like what we have today the wind would shave you as well as frequent showers of rain. Perhaps they have better weather tho'. Mrs Kiernan sent Mrs Seery a letter. She got from Cousin Mary Kelly C Town three large sheets like this I wish I could fill a few pages of a nice letter now for my dear little man but no such luck as to be able to give that much pleasure. So I need not try but I will send you lots of love & kiss
From your loving
May

19th April

My dear James
    I am awfully sorry you were disappointed this morn but as you will see It was not my fault I wrote yesterday & got no chance to post. I am going to Mullingar now & I will post my self- I don't mean I'll put myself in the box but I'll put the letter- I have no extra news except how delighted Louis is with himself says he is just as happy as James Finn ever was Johnnie C. is getting very very low in himself the first bad signs he has ever shown so that he is taking a lot of the pleasure out of Louis's engagement for Mrs S I am going to see about that costume piece perhaps I might see something I would like better. I suppose we can expect you by the late train Thursday no chance of your mother coming with you I

suppose I have no news at all so good-bye I hope you will excuse
me for disappointing you & excuse this scribble too
   Very best wishes & warmest love
   From your loving
   May

   My dearest and best
      I was overjoyed to get your letter this morning as I came
down to breakfast with the most gloomy forebodings. I had been
worrying overnight about that trouble you got off the table and
conjuring up pictures of the injuries you got turning out more
serious than you had supposed with the result that you were
very ill. The result was that I was looking out for the post from
my window while I was dressing. I missed seeing him coming to
my door but I saw him going to the next house and concluded
that there was no letter for me I came down therefore in a very
gloomy mood quite determined to wire as soon as I got down
and to leave for Castletown by the afternoon train unless I got a
satisfactory wire in reply. My relief was very great as you can easily understand when I read your letter and saw there was nothing
wrong. As I told you in my letter yesterday I shall be down by the
evening train and hope to see my darling about half past seven.
We were all delighted to see that Louis had got on so well and
was so pleased with himself and with his girl. It's a great blessing that he will be settled any how especially before the father
sails out as there might be rows between Stanny[60] and himself if
they were both in Markethill together. He must be very pleased
indeed with himself when he compares his happiness to mine
but I hardly think that it will come up to the high water mark that
I have reached. However it shows you that people generally are
inclined to think I am a lucky chap to pull off the first prize when
they take me as a standard of happiness. I hope I'll live to deserve
my happiness anyhow with God's help and yours, my dear.
I have absolutely nothing to say except that I love my dearest
May with all the strength I have. I send you my warmest love as
ever
   Your ever loving James

The final prenuptial visit was planned for the Easter weekend
1916, so James must have left Dublin on Good Friday 21st
April. The Dublin James returned to was in turmoil. On Easter
Monday 24th April, the Rising had begun. By Saturday the
29th surrender had been declared. The surrender document
read: "In order to prevent the further slaughter of Dublin
citizens, and in the hope of saving the lives of our followers
now surrounded and hopelessly outnumbered, the members
of the Provisional Government present at headquarters have
agreed to an unconditional surrender, and the commandants
of the various districts in the City and County will order their
their commands to lay down arms."

The rebel headquarters was located at the General Post Office (GPO) where James Connolly, overall military command-
er and four other members of the Military Council: Patrick
Pearse, Tom Clarke, Seán Mac Dermott and Joseph Plunkett
were located. After occupying the Post Office, the Volunteers
hoisted two republican flags and Pearse read a Proclamation
of the Republic.Elsewhere, rebel forces took up positions at
the Four Courts, the centre of the Irish legal establishment,
at Jacob's Biscuit Factory and Boland's Mill and at the hospital complex at South Dublin Union and the adjoining Distill-
ery at Marrowbone Lane. Another contingent, under Michael
Mallin, dug in on St. Stephen's Green. However, although it
was lightly guarded, Volunteer and Citizen Army forces under
Seán Connolly failed to take Dublin Castle, the centre of British rule in Ireland and Trinity College. One major battle was
at Mount Street Bridge right next to James' workplace.

The GPO was the only major rebel post to be physically taken
back during the week. The others surrendered only after
Pearse's surrender order, carried by nurse named Elizabeth
O'Farrell, reached them. Sporadic fighting therefore contin-
ued until Sunday, when word of the surrender reached the
other rebel garrisons. Command of British forces had passed
from Lowe to General John Maxwell, who arrived in Dublin
just in time to take the surrender. Maxwell was made temporary military governor of Ireland.

?29th April⁶²

The Mullingar Motor Company Ltd
OPEN AND CLOSED MOTOR CARS ALWAYS FOR HIRE

My Darling May,

I got back all right and found my mother and Essie quite well but frightened. We had some trouble in getting out of Mullingar had to get a military permit which however was never asked for. I had first to go to Drumcondra with a lady who was my fellow passenger and I was much delayed in consequence as I had to go back round by Lucan to get in by Terenure. In Drumcondra I ran up against a friend who told me that the volunteers had just surrendered on promise of an amnesty and I believe from what I hear now it is true that they have surrendered. I really have nothing to say except to thank God that I found everything quite well at home. No news upon Moll or Nora but I hope in God and feel quite confident that they are quite safe. The driver is taking this back but as he is only leaving now at 7pm he may be late for the messenger from Togherstown. If he is late I will get him to post this tomorrow in Mullingar. I need hardly tell you how I thank God for His goodness to me in all things.

    With heartfelt love and blessings
    James

Give my regards and heartfelt thanks to Mrs Seery
    James

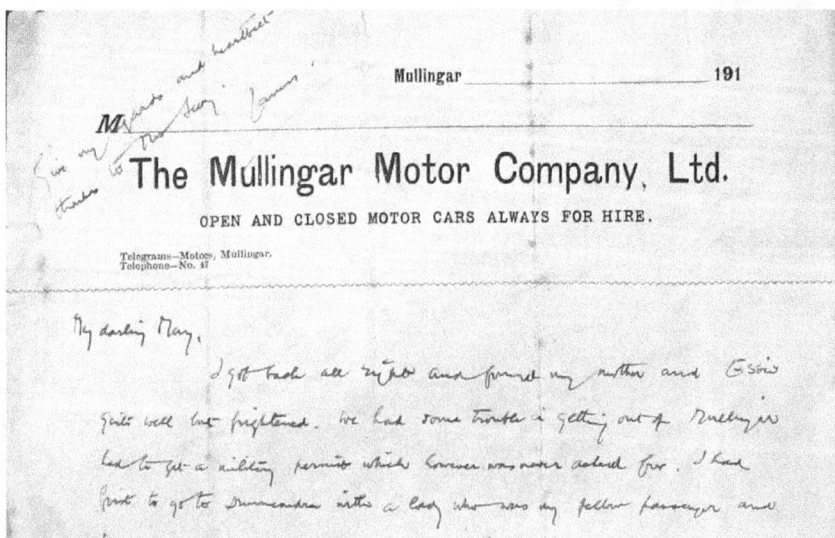

39 Belgrave Square
Rathmines
Dublin
3rd May 1916

My darling May,
Everyone is all right here thank God. Nora & Moll arrived back quite safe from the North last evening but they had to drive on an outsider from Malahide where they spent Monday night. Mother is quite well but still upset by events. Things are getting normal but there is still a certain amount of sniping from houses at night, owing to stray men who have not surrendered and who are apparently determined to hold out to the last.

We heard on Monday that the Volunteers had captured Mullingar Station on Saturday evening but I suppose there is no truth in that. Give my regards to everyone and with warmest and dearest love to my sweetest and best girl

AROUND RATHMINES

ANXIETY ABOUT FOOD SUPPLY.

In Rathmines district, although there was comparative immunity from the more violent scenes witnessed in the city and other parts, excitement and tension were very high through the week. Being a residential locality in which a great number of people live, who carry on business in the city, the fact that hundreds were compelled to remain altogether out of the city day after day added greatly to the demand for food. And, in addition to this, numbers of people who reside in the city made their way to Rathmines in search of provisions as their usual marketing streets were rendered unsafe by the military operations and constant firing. In consequence of these demands on the resources of the suburban shopkeepers, exciting scenes were witnessed as people struggled in crowds outside bakeries in the endeavour to purchase even a small quantity of bread by hook or by crook.

Ever your loving
James

Togherstown
Ballinea
Mullingar
7th ~~April~~ *May 1916*

My dearest James

In case you might not have received my last letter I write again and as well I feel in better form writing to you because I imagine I'm talking, still there are a lot of big long things I never would face to write although I write on as I think to you regardless of my letter shapes and other things that I'm sure do jar on you sometimes but I'm too old now to be taught I'm afraid

Mrs Seery got both your cards and as well as all ourselves she was delighted to know all was well with all in 39 so far but of course your mother's invitation for Sat was late but it was very severe weather in any case.

I have felt a little done up since the Sat you left I don't know was it the anxiety or what but I sent Gerald in on Sunday morn instead of Sat night, he got your letter and it gave me great relief but news was so very scarce and uncertain that I very soon began to look out for another letter, it's sickening not to know how long that suspense would last but it did not last too long the blood shed seems to have got on my ....(page missing)

39 Belgrave Square
Rathmines
Dublin
8th May 1916

My dearest dearest May,

I was delighted to get your letter this morning. I had very little expectation of hearing from you for another day or two although I was half hoping I might see Mrs Seery and yourself. My mother wrote to her last week asking her and yourself to come up and I thought that perhaps you could both have managed. We had a letter from Mrs Seery this morning also saying that she would come up during this week and that you would probably come also. I hope in God I may see you this week. Indeed part of the time I feared that I might never see you again. You remember how often I told you that both by letter and by mouth: that I might not have the good fortune or the grace from God to be married to you. Now somehow I feel that I may be thought worthy although why it should be so I cannot understand when I think of all the fine spirits that this calamity has called to their eternal account. Things are gradually getting more like their usual way and people generally are beginning to rebuild and restore all that has been shattered but it will be many a long day before Dublin is anything like its old self. It will probably take 10 years before the central parts are completely restored.

Hope everyone at home is well and that you were not too anxious for your worthless husband-to-be during the past week. I am writing you a postcard also in case this letter is delayed by the censor. Give my regards to everyone and with fondest and warmest love

Your loving
James

39 Belgrave Square

Dublin after the Easter rising

Rathmines
Dublin
10th May 1916

My dearest love,

You are a darling to write to me again yesterday. I was not expecting a letter of course and was delighted when I got home yesterday evening to hear from my mother that there was a letter waiting for me. It must have arrived yesterday after I left for the office. The post is very erratic these times for example there is no post for the night mail after 3pm. So I have to write to you immediately after I come into the office or I shall miss it. However we have been so long without mails that we bless the lost offices for any little convenience at all now. I was overjoyed to see that we may look forward to the pleasure of seeing you on Saturday. I need hardly tell you with what anxiety and eagerness I am waiting for the moment when I can embrace my dearest and best girl again and thank God for being thought worthy to live to see her again. I hope that the trouble through which we have all passed will eventually bring good to our poor country and that it will with God's blessing make me a better man and a more worthy one for the dear good true girl who loves me. I hope you heard from Jennie since and that all is well with them in Mitchelstown. They are still arresting men all over the country and I suppose you know that they have shot twelve of the leaders in the last week. They are P.H. Pearse and his brother Willy Pearse, Tom Clarke (an old fenian), Thos McDonagh, J.Plunket (a son of Count Plunket), Major McBride (of the South African War), Eamonn Kent, Conn Colbert, J.J. Heuston, M. Mallon and one or two others whose names I forget at the moment. A large number (up to 40 I think) have got penal servitude ranging from 3 to 20 years; Countess Markievitz imprisoned for life and 200 or 300 prisoners taken to England to be interred etc.

Those executed after the Rising

I had a letter from Johnnie today and of course I'll go round and see them at Callaghans about the job there. I will write to him tomorrow but don't mention it to him unless of course he has

T. J. GALLAGHAN & CO., LTD.
13, 14, 15, 16 DAME STREET
BEG TO INFORM THEIR CUS-
TOMERS AND THE PUBLIC
THAT BUSINESS IS BEING
CARRIED ON AS USUAL.
THEIR EXTENSIVE PREMISES
AND LARGE STOCKS BEING
ABSOLUTELY INTACT, ALL
ORDERS FOR TAILORING, SAD-
DLERY, AND GENERAL OUT-
FITTING CAN BE EXECUTED
IMMEDIATELY.

already told you that he is looking for a job there. We are in the middle of tradesmen this week papering etc. But we hope to be in some sort of order by Saturday when we shall have the pleasure of welcoming your-self and Mrs Seery to Belgrave Square. Tell Mrs S. to bring up my bag and belongings if she doesn't mind the trouble. Let me know what train you are coming on and I will meet you at the station or thereabouts. I'm not sure whether I can get into the station or not but will find out and let you know tomorrow. Give my warmest regards to your mother, Nano, Mrs. Seery and everyone and with fondest love and kisses

Your ever loving
James

Togherstown
Ballinea
Mullingar
10ᵗʰ May 1916

My dearest James

I was very glad to get your letter yesterday I did not get card you said you were sending but I was delighted to see all goes well with you all. I am anxiously looking forward to seeing you next Sat. I don't know yet what train I expect the best part of the day will be spent in the train I believe they are very slow we are only staying the week end so we must only thank God for that same. We are always looking out for the paper & news we manage to get an odd paper now & then but I saw where all Civil Servants[62] were to render an account of their Easter holidays, will you not be asked to render an account of all the time you spent talking to me & sitting at Fay's fire. You need not be afraid

to mention our names anyway; we are not very rebellious charac-
ters. I have not a word of news. I hope you got my letter posted
Monday.

Good bye now with fondest hopes of seeing you soon
Your everloving May

National Health Insurance Commission (Ireland)
Pembroke House
Upper Mount Street
Dublin
11ᵗʰ May 1916

My dearest love,
        Thanks ever so much for letter received this evening. The
postman's knock was a very pleasant sound after the very un-
pleasant sounds that have been in our ears for some time past.
I haven't been able to get to find out whether the Broadstone is
open to non-travellers or what time the train from Castletown ar-
rives but I shall be waiting for you either in or outside the station
on Saturday long before the train is likely to arrive. I tried twice
today to get the Broadstone on the telephone to make enquiries
but failed each time. We only got the telephones back from the
military a day or two ago and I think they are still in bad order.
We are all in a mess at home for the past few days with painting,
paperhanging etc. but the house will be very much improved, I'm
sure, when the job is done. We will be in a somewhat better position on Saturday to welcome you both as a good part of the dirty
work will be completed by then and part of the house anyway will
have its best smile on to welcome its mistress. I must corner Mrs
Seery when she is up and settle the long-outstanding question of
the best man. I suppose I had better make all the arrangements
now for the 7th June as a certainty. I'm uncertain whether it will
be possible as all to go on a prolonged honeymoon in the South
then as I suppose that railway and hotel arrangements etc. are
upset but I will enquire anyhow and be able to tell you on Saturday. I see in this morning's paper a list of a batch of prisoners
from Mitchelstown district. I don't see the name of John Corbett
amongst them but I notice a man called Roche. I suppose he's
hardly one of the family. I must close this now as Duffy is waiting
for me to go to lunch. I send you as always my fondest and warm-

est love and in fancy I kiss your dear face
   Your ever loving James

                                                                16th May 1916

   My dearest May
      I have only time for a line to say that I wrote to Pat Moran today asking him to be my best man. I haven't yet written to the brother, Father Frank, to ask him to do the job for me but I suppose it is the usual and natural thing to do and I suppose people would talk and say there was a row between us if I didn't ask him. What does your mother and yourself think of it? I suppose however that neither of you has any particular opinion or preference one way or the other about it. I hope you both got home safe and sound and found everyone well and that the cat didn't eat the kitchen tongs in the interval. How does Gerald like his new mirror? Has he started shaving yet? When you see Mrs Seery (which will be I presume within the next week or so) will you ask her whether Johnnie wants me to call on those people in Pims etc. she was talking about and if so let me have their names and addresses. You'll be glad to hear that John Fitzgerald (one of our men here) who was arrested last week has been released today and will be back again on duty in a day or so. I think I was telling you about him having been arrested at his house in Iona Road. One or two others have had their houses searched but nothing incriminating was discovered. No strange news in the papers this morning beyond what you saw in last evening's papers.
   Give my regards to all and with warmest and fondest love to my dearest girl
      Ever your loving and devoted James

IRISH PRISONERS
DEPORTED.

The following is a list of 273 prisoners, who were removed from Richmond Barracks on May 12th, and lodged in Wakefield Detention Barracks on the 13th :—

National Health Insurance Commission (Ireland)
Pembroke House
Upper Mount Street
Dublin

My dearest May,
      I intended writing to you yesterday but I couldn't manage even five minutes all the morning and as the post still closes at 3pm, it was too late when I managed to have a few minutes to myself in the evening. John Fitzgerald was in the office yesterday for a while accounting for his experiences in prison. The only charge against him was that he "spoke Irish continually in his house and played Irish and German music on his piano" and his neighbour, a man named Casey over 50 years of age, was charged that " between the 22nd April and 1st May he was seen speaking to people who were believed to be Sinn Féiners". Absolutely nothing else on the charge sheet of either party and although they were kept in prison for five days, they were never examined or called upon to answer any charge whatsoever. Both were released on Friday morning. They slept 25 in one room on the floor with one blanket each and neither chair, table, pillow, knife, fork spoon or any other means of making themselves clean or comfortable. When they wanted to sit down they could sit on their grug. He tells me also that there were 7 men in all shot without trial in Portobello Barracks, that is Sheehy- Skeffington and 6 others and that Skeffington was not shot by a firing party but by a Captain Colthurst (one of the Colthursts of Cork) by his own hands with a revolver.. I haven't seen any news of the Casement trial worth relating. Up to the present the only evidence produced was the usual tall yarns about his founding an Irish Brigade in Germany and his landing at Ardfort. About Father Moran, I will write to him today asking him to do the job

Francis Sheehy-Skeffington

for us. Why do you hope it will go off all right? I'm quite sure now that we will be right after all the dangers and troubles we have all been through and I am trusting therefore in God's goodness that for some reason or other I have been thought worthy to be married to you. We were all delighted to hear about Johnnie's journey and hope that his troubles are now over. Glad to hear that you are all busy with the spuds. This weather is grand for all the spring work. How did you manage to get the pains in your legs? Aren't you very silly to be running the risk of getting your death of cold? I'll have to take better care of you than you do of yourself when I get possession of you. No news otherwise except that we are nearly evicted out of the house these days with the painters Regards to all and with fondest and dearest love to my dear & darling

Ever your loving
James.

39 Belgrave Square
Rathmines
Dublin
19th May 1916

My dearest May,

I go your watch from Hopkins all right yesterday on giving your name care of Mr Finn. There was nothing wrong with it they tell me except that it required adjustment. I don't know what that means but in any case it is going all right now and I hope it will continue to do so. Don't forget to put it on an hour on Sunday evening in accordance with the Daylight saving. You'll have Mass in Loughnavally in future on alternate Sundays at 7:30 (real time) so even your mother will be put to the pin of her collar to be on time unless she makes the necessary changes in her timepieces. I got a letter from Pat Moran this morning to say that he will act as best man for me with pleasure so I have that much fixed up anyhow. By the way I would like very much to ask Father Willie Moran[63] to the marriage in addition to Father Frank if your mother would not mind. I am afraid that the accommodation may be somewhat restricted and if it gives her any inconvenience I'll not ask him but would be glad to hear from you. The guests from my side of the house would then be four at the <u>most</u> viz Fathers Frank & Willie Moran, Pat Moran and Nora. Probably Nora may not be able to go and perhaps Father Willie also but in any case it won't be more than four. If that number would be inconvenient let me know when you are writing. By the way about wedding presents for Nano and yourself, I was thinking of getting bangles or something of that sort for both of you. What do you think would Nano like also yourself. I'd like to know that also soon. No news at all. Dan Moran called to see us yesterday evening you know he is Father Willies brother. He was in the Volunteers but was not called up.

Regards to all and fondest and truest love to yourself.

Always your loving and devoted

James

20*th* *May 1916*

My darling May,

I have very little to say to you today except the things that I suppose you are tired of hearing and that you can guess at even when I don't tell you. I need only say on that score that every day that brings us nearer to the 7th June makes me more impatient for the moment when I can have you for myself. I hope you got the watch alright this morning and that it will give better satisfaction than I fear the donor ever will give you. By the way, will you please keep safely the box in which I sent you the watch. It is not of very much intrinsic value as you can see but my mother attaches a great deal of sentimental value to it and wishes to have it back. You needn't send it back; I can bring it back with me on the eventful day. I have been enquiring again about the holiday arrangements on the Great Southern and think they will be all right by the time our little "hurroo" comes off. Things here are settling down more and more every day. The papers are still full of a settlement on the Home Rule question and I hear on very good authority indeed that it is a settled thing that Home Rule is to come into operation without delay. That will mean big changes and you might see your little man Prime Minister yet. Jokes apart I believe there will be very interesting happenings in Ireland in the course of the next few months and I don't think they will be to the disadvantage of the country generally.

We haven't heard or seen anything of Johnnie since he left for Cork. Mrs Seery was saying if he came back he would stop a night

with us so I am hoping from the fact that we haven't seen him that he has got on well. Tell Mrs Seery that I got my "weskit[64]" all right and that I intend to wear it for my wedding I don't see what better I can get unless I turn up in a morning coat and a silk hat. What do you think? If you would prefer me to get something darker and smarter, I will do so with pleasure. No news since from the O'Connors, but their cousins, Eddy Cox and his father have been deported to England I expect you heard us talk of the Coxs. I send you my warmest and most devoted love as ever,
    Your loving,
    James

22th May 1916

My dearest and best,
    I got your letter yesterday and was of course delighted as usual to hear from my dearest girl. I had intended writing yesterday but Teresa Jones came in on us in the evening and put it out of my power to write. I'm glad that you have eventually decided on how your dress is to be made but I think if you don't look very snappy they'll leave you in the lurch in Keelan's and maybe I'd have to marry you without a rag on you.!

As regards that however of course you could always turn up smiling with your watch wristlet and your bangle and to be in the fashion with you I could appear in a tall hat and a pair of cuffs on my ankles like any African Chief. I must look after the bangle and brooch this week but I don't know where to go now that Hopkin's has disappeared off the map[65]. As regards myself I think I'll buy a tie pin or something of that sort and

BURNING OF SACKVILLE STREET.

Thus the fight went on day and night. On Thursday night a heavy bombardment was directed against Messrs. Hopkins' establishment, which was full of Sinn Feiners. When the house was being brought down about them, as many of the rebels as could escape fled in the direction of the Post Office, only to meet their death in the streets. Fire then added its terrors to the awful scene, and in a short time the whole block of buildings from Hopkins' corner up to Lower Abbey street was like a furnace. The members of the hard-worked and courageous Fire Brigade made their best endeavour to extinguish the fire, but no human agency could have arrested its progress. Onward it swept, one house after another enveloped.

you can even pay for it when we meet again. I'm glad that your
mother doesn't mind my inviting Father Willie Moran. Of course
I'm not at all sure that he can come but he may be able especially
as he has a motorbike that will take him to and from fairly easily.
I hope that your fears that your mother will be called away will
not come off. It would be a rotten thing if we had to postpone the
marriage now after all our disappointments. Johnnie Cunningham turned up on Saturday evening well pleased with his visit to
Cork; he seems to think it fairly certain but is unwilling to be too
confident for fear of another failure. Don't worry about my being
arrested. There is no fear now or indeed at any time. If I was any
blooming good I'd have been arrested long ago. Men a thousand
times better have a daisy quilt over them in Glasnevin now.
Poor Rody O'Connor has been deported to England but Seán is
still confined in Richmond Barracks. My mother was over seeing
them yesterday. They are having six soldiers billeted on them
from today, I suppose by way of punishment. Pleasant thing to
have six boyos in your best rooms for goodness knows how long.
I have no other news so will close with heartfelt love and kisses to
my darling May
    Your ever loving
    James

Togherstown
Undated ? 22nd may 1916

    My dearest James
        Many thanks for your letter of yesterday you don't forget
your promise of letting me have a letter for Sunday & I am very
glad
I am just after leaning down my paintbrush to write this I am very
busy painting I want to leave all the painting and sewing done
before I say good-bye to my real interests in the house of course
I will always take a great interest in it still not the same when I
have a house of my own.
Well as I told you I was in Mullingar on Saturday I decided on the
make of my dress & hat the blouse will be like (in a way) Jennies
as you see it in her photo with the under blouse a very pale pink
to match my hat of pale pale pink the pink goes well with the sea
blue although pink was never my colour still it did not seem to

clash. It looked very nice the general rig out as I saw it however it
will look when all is finished certainly the colours are a splendid
contrast however the wearer will figure with them
I met a cousin of my Mothers Mrs Paul Murtagh[66] a stepmother
to Dowey(?) you met in Mrs Seery's & Mrs Jack Kelly the Glebe.
she seemed to know you & wished to be remembered to you, I
forget where she said she had met you. Mrs Seery had a pc from
Johnnie this morning with the words: please meet me at the 7.30
train- that is the only news he sent her except a telegram since he
went. I think she is very hot about it. Her father is giving in to give
the money to Louis so she is very contented on that front I have
not a word more of news so goodbye
      Your loving old girl
      May

                                                          23rd May, 1916

      My dearest love,
            I'm not going to write you much today for I haven't got a
minute handy to spare but I don't like to let the day pass without
letting you know I have been thinking of you. I got your letter all
right and was interested in the details of the wedding dress I can't
say that I understand them very clearly. All the same I expect I'll
be able to tell you pretty decidedly whether I like it or not so God
help you if it is not becoming. I'm sure all the same that my dearest girl will look very well.
I wish to goodness I could hope that I will look something like
the sort of bridegroom that you ought to have. I know very well
that everyone that sees us together will be saying to themselves
"What could this nice young girl have seen in that ould cod to
induce her to marry him". I was amused with your account of the
bould Johnnie and his news from Cork. He's a cool sort all right
and I wouldn't be much surprised if he forgot Mrs Seery's goodness to him very quickly if he once got back into a safe job again.
However I suppose that's only human nature and I expect I should
be as ungrateful myself as the next one. It doesn't do for people
in glass houses to throw stones. I was delighted to hear about
Louis but the father took the good out of it like the British Government and Home Rule. Must shut up, no more time. Warmest
and dearest love to my own good little girl

From your loving
James

Togherstown
Ballinea
25th May 1916

My dearest James
Many thanks for your letter this morning. I need not tell you how delighted I was to get copy of Pearce's letter. Johnnie had told me you had it & I must say I was feeling a bit jealous you never told me about it but it seems you did not think me alto-gether wanting in interest in such things I am sending Jennie a copy of it.
By an article I saw (on I don't know what paper) I have great hopes Casement will turn catholic that would be grand I say a special prayer for his conversion always.
We could easily order the car if you wished you need not worry about the car for me. Mother will see about one, but only for the fashion of it. I think it is foolish to take a car out for Mullingar to bring me up to Loughnavally
I have great sympathy with your Mother to have the house so long upset Johnnie said there was difficulty in getting the paper. You should have got one like me. I did cealing (sic) & walls and left the room pretty square in one afternoon the cealing turned out beautiful & white but that was only a chance if it was black it was all the same I would only give it the one coat
This is a very wet day here I hope we will have a better day for our marriage. Mrs Seery told me to tell your Mother she would have written only waiting to have some news of Johnnie she (Mrs S) is gone to pro reception for Bab Lemmon[67] today
Good bye now dearest James
Best love from your loving
May
I forgot to ask you how you came by the copy of Pearce's letter. I am returning with many thanks

My Dearest Mother,
I have been hoping up to now it would be possible to see
you again, but it does not seem possible. Good-bye dear,
dear, mother. Through you I say good-bye to 'Wow Wow,'
(a sister), Mary, Brigid, Willie, Miss B. Miceal, cousin Mag-
gine and everyone at St. Enda's. I hope and believe Willie
and the St. Enda boys will be all safe.
I have written two papers about financial affairs and one
about my books which I want you to get. With them are
a few poems which I want added to the poems in MS in
my bookcase. You asked me to write a little poem which
would seem to be said by you about me. I have written it,
and a copy is in Arbour Hill Barracks with other papers and
Father Aloysius is taking care of another copy of it.
I have just received Holy Communion. I am happy, except
for the great grief of parting from you. This is the death I
should have asked for if God had given me the choice of all
deaths - to die a soldier's death for Ireland and for free-
dom. We have done right. People will say hard things of us
now, but later on they will praise us. Do not grieve for all
this but think of it as a sacrifice which God has asked of me
and of you.
Good-bye again, dear mother. May God bless you for your
great love for me and for your great faith, and may He
remember all you have so bravely suffered. I hope soon
to see papa, and in a little while we shall all be together
again. I have not words to tell you of my love for you and
how my heart yearns to you all. I will call to you in my
heart at the last moment.
Your son Pat

Kilmainham Prison, Pearse's Last Letter – May 3rd, 1916.
Copies of this were widely distributed in the months following his execution.

National Health Insurance Commission (Ireland)
Pembroke house
Upper Mount Street
Dublin
26th May 1916

My dearest May

Thank you very much for your letter of this morning. I received the copy of Pearce's letter quite safely and am glad you were not so foolish as to think I didn't send it because I thought you incapable of understanding it. I sent it to you as a human document and not as a political one and I know very well that in anything where genuine sentiment and capacity for self-sacrifice are concerned you are a much better and appreciative judge than I am. Apart from that I am quite aware that you have at least your share of brains (to say the least of it) and I am not such a supercilious "high – brow" as to imagine that in that respect I am at all superior to you. The real reason why I didn't send the letter sooner is that I had only the one copy, I was too lazy to copy it and I wanted to show it to one or two people before parting with it. So there's the whole of the story and I hope you are satisfied with my explanation. I am surprised Johnnie hasn't heard anything yet but I suppose a week or so will settle it. Thanks very much for your offer to order motor for me. I expect Pat Moran tomorrow and if he doesn't turn up I shall avail of your services. It's very nice to have a little wife willing to do jobs for one. I have no news at all so will close with warmest love and kisses

Your ever loving
James

And just this moment see an Army Zeppelin cruising over our heads here in Merrion Square. It's not a German one though so you needn't be alarmed.

National Health Insurance Commission (Ireland)
Pembroke house
Upper Mount Street
Dublin
27th May 1916

My dearest May,

I wonder what I'm going to write about today. My mind seems to be an absolute blank so far as news is concerned except perhaps the yarns and rumours of all kinds that are going about Dublin at present. I suppose you have heard that we are going to have another rebellion on Whit Monday.

The rumour has been around Dublin for the last fortnight and I believe priests have been advising people to be very circumspect during the Whitsuntide holidays and to keep near the "shelter" etc. You will observe it is to break out just after our marriage and we shall probably be right in the middle of it in the County Kerry so you had better start saying your prayers for both of us and don't be wasting your breath over Sir Roger Casement's conversion. What's the good of my keeping a wife if she is going to neglect her poor husband that wants all the prayers she can say.

I have been enquiring at Hopkin's about bangles and the brooch for Nano. The most of their stuff has gone in the week but they will be able to let me see a selection of bangles on Monday.

As to the brooch, I was thinking of getting Nano something on the Tara brooch style but I'm afraid they are not to be obtained hardly in Dublin now. Hopkins were practically the only makers and all their stocks of such brooches and also the dies for making them have I hear been destroyed. I'll see what I can do however but perhaps she would prefer some other design.

Let me know on that point by Monday if possible. If she likes stones, let me know the colour etc. As regards yourself do you prefer a chain bracelet bangle or a solid bracelet? If the former is it a curb chain or a fancy chain? I suggest the fancy chain as the curb chain is a bit common I think. If you prefer a solid bracelet would you like it with stones and if so what colour? Hope the dress is getting on well and will turn out as big a success as the wearer. I fancy I can see my dear dear girl looking a picture in it and I long to kiss her sweet face.

I hope that God will bless us both. I hope you are praying for me because I need it so badly. I have no other news at all so will say goodbye with warmest and most devoted love

Your ever loving

James

Togherstown
Ballinea
Mullingar
Co W Meath
29th May 1916

My dearest James

Very many thanks for your letter of yesterday and today you are very good to write so often I must give you something nice for your goodness in that way when I see you. We had Fr Donellon this morning with Mass he brought me "my paper" too he had your name on it- Jacobo he called you wasn't that a shame. I asked Nano about brooch, she only laughed but I think she'd like red stones, she said tho' whatever you liked yourself I think I'd prefer a fancy bracelet (chain) to a solid one, and about the size of the ring I'm afraid you will have to send me a card I don't see any other way I suppose it would not do to send a porter bottle that was the only suggestion Nano could make.

The poor British seem to be getting enough of it at present- however it will end will the subjects have to pay the piper- of course they are doing so already but if the land is taxed it will leave all trade going east.

I was yesterday evening standing outside of the door when I saw a lady coming walking up the avenue who was it but Jocie Casey she had left Miss & Mrs Moran at the gate we were glad to see her, she gave us a particular invitation to go over before I'd get married I never saw a girl to improve in appearance dress & manner as much as Jocie in fact I never saw her well-dressed before, she had been to see Agnes⁶⁸ (Mrs Nicholas Duffy) She didn't call to see John or Mary said they thought themselves too grand for her and Annie the nun in Cork didn't write to her for Christmas, too grand also, in that case it's the grand that are to be pitied more than the common. I am going to Mullingar tomorrow to see about dress I'll see about car for you how long would you want it for would it take the day what time would we want to leave this about?

Johnnie heard nothing since. Gerald heard talking of the French being beaten at Verdun, he was afterwards seen trespassing in the hall with a dirty spade, when he was asked where he was

bound for he said to bury the Allies. A big undertaking!
I don't think I have any news so I'll finish with warmest love &
wishes
   from your loving May

National Health Insurance Commission (Ireland)
Pembroke House
Upper Mount Street
Dublin
30th May 1916

   My dearest May
        I was very much disappointed at not receiving a letter
today as I was anxious to settle the matter of the bangle and
also the even more important matter if the wedding ring. I was
looking at a few specimens of the latter at Hopkin's temporary
place yesterday[69]; they have succeeded in saving a few from the
fire and I rather liked one which was rather thick and heavy and
generally massive looking. I'm not sure whether you might not
like a ring somewhat less imposing and if you do of course your
wish is law. But I want to know the size anyway and if you haven't
written by today will you please drop me a line tomorrow when
you get this.
We had Father Willie Moran up to see us yesterday and he stayed
last night. He had no special news although he was full of the
Rebellion and the incidents of it. There was a very hot correspondence published in the Cork Examiner on Saturday last between
General Sir John Maxwell and Edward Thomas, Bishop of Limer-
ick, in which I believe the latter referred to the appeals England
made for clemency to the Boer Government for Jameson at the
time of the Jameson Raid and contrasted that with the want of
clemency shown in Ireland. He referred also to the "bloody and
fatuous" policy of Maxwell since his arrival in Ireland. I haven't
been able to see a copy of the Examiner yet: I believe all the copies that could be traced were seized by the military. Maybe Jennie
would have a copy in Mitchelstown. If so you might be able to ask
her for it as I believe it is worth reading. Please drop me a line by
return as I must get ring this week. With warmest love and kisses
   Your ever loving
   James

Togherstown
Undated ? 31ˢᵗ may 1916

My dearest James

I got your letter this morning I am sure you were expecting a letter from me, but the post leaving "advance time[70]" & the
men working by old time leaves the post gone before they even
quit, as you will see I had a letter written on Monday & posted it
in Mullingar yesterday- We had a nice day in town- better than
today anyway I had my dress fitted it looks very well I think &
my hat also but I can tell you I was very sick of the job of turning
& twisting & standing all the time while being fitted We settled
about a motor, booked one for me and for you he said any car
he'd send would be all right he'll charge by the mile so he could
not say what either would come to. We could not let him know
the hour at the time but you can tell him Tuesday night when you
arrive in Mullingar I suppose 8.30 old time would be about the
hour, would that suit you let me know & it will be all right what
time will we have to leave this at do you know?
I think we won't fast that morning I mean for Holy Communion
the drive would be very long for you we can go on Sunday before
instead like the woman going to Mass on Sat instead of Sunday
About the ring I asked you to send me the card although a hole I
would make myself in a card would do full as well I suppose but
about the ring itself- I know I never could wear any but the two
rings on that one finger so whether it be large or small I don't
know which would be the best. I think I will leave it to your taste
I liked your taste in the watch & as well you have the advantage
of having seen both the ring and the finger I dare say unless you
have a great eye & memory altogether you forget my ring finger
is fat and short I got my first present yesterday from Mrs Keer-
nan. A Silver tea pot I hope you will get something nice for yourself
We did not see the Cork Examiner and Jennie always sends it to
us when there is anything in it she must not have got it but I will
ask her. I heard that Bulfin[71] was in the GPO & in uniform so he
cannot get off so easy I have no more news so good-bye. I hope
we won't have weather like this for our wedding whatever about
the honeymoon

Best love from your loving
May

Togherstown
Ballinea
Mullingar
Co W Meath
1ˢᵗ June 1916

My dearest James

I got your letter this morn also card to fit ring and a paper I think addressed by your Mother we were very glad to get it and see Dr Dwyer's letters to Maxwell I wonder they got on papers at all they were very good. We are having awful weather hear (sic) at present quiet (sic) cold as well as wet. I hope they are trying to spit up all the bad weather before we go off.

Christy is gone to Mullingar today & will take home all my dress etc. nearly, so they won't be late at that rate. Mrs Seery was called over to Balrath last night, the boss there was at death's door with drink but is slowly recovering Mrs Kiernan had got word from Gertie Duffy saying if she went to Dublin with her to see the Doctors she would pay her expenses for one day. I believe she is very delicate (Gertie) but does not think it, like every one of her said complaint, people all pity John- the take in he got- but I think one is as much to be pitied as the other

I am returning the ring card size T is my size About your present I will look at some things in Mullingar if I don't get something I think you would like I will wait till we go to Cork won't that be all right

Well Christy has not gone to Mullingar at all, there were arrangements made to drive the filly & Mrs S pressed her car & son, also when Christy went down he asked the loan of the bit from Tom, he got it and threw it on the ground to him & they were all giving him short answers, he that so seldom goes near them so he did not go, with the going on they had he'd be late for Mass there. The whole cause of the general bad humour was a letter Johnnie had got saying that firm was not going to be opened for the present & they therefore did not require him it was hard of course after such long wait for both parties but I can't understand them showing temper to Christy that would give them the house from over his head.

I am sure tho' like ourselves ye will be disappointed for Johnnies job,

I have no more news now dearest James I hope you will get to make out this, I would not be half as mad if it were myself it was done because I have "gift of the gab"

warmest love from your loving

May

[I couldn't get a chance of posting this. It's by old time the boys stop work they are at a particular & ugly job now shearing so I hope my poor little man won't be disappointed too much. I was thinking since your present seem like a present at all still I think there is nothing I could get for you would like or want if you could suggest anything I would like to get it but if you would only like the tie pin it would be better get it yourself for I am afraid I wouldn't know much about such a thing]

1st June 1916

My dearest love

You'll have to let me off with a very short note today as I am awfully rushed and have been all day, partly business and partly arrangements for coming events. Glad you fixed up the motor for me and am much obliged for your good offices in the matter. About the ring, I think what I have selected will be all right and I don't think it will look too imposing. In any case you're worthy of the best I can get for you. The time you suggest will of course suit me that is 9:30 new time but remember we shall have to catch train at Portarlington at 4 o'clock new time and I presume will have to leave Togherstown about 2 pm. That will however give us plenty of time I think.

Tourist arrangements in the South are all off I'm afraid so we must try and manage as best we can by car as the motor coaches will not be running until 1st July. We will make for Glengariff anyhow and chance our arm from there as to getting on to Killarney by the coast route. I haven't time to write any more now although I could spend a few more minutes anyhow telling you how I love you. Do you need me to do that though? I hope that by

now you know me enough to feel sure of my sentiments in that respect anyhow. Don't forget ring card this evening.

I send you my warmest love and kisses, my dear dear May
Your loving
James

Shall go to Holy Communion on Sunday as you suggest. Please remember me in yours and pray remember me in yours and pray hard for me. I kiss you again

James

The Marriage

They married on June 7th 1916 in Loughnavally, Fr Frank Moran officiated, Patrick Moran was best man, Nano Fay was bridesmaid. It seems like they honeymooned in the South of Ireland.

And then they settled down to married life. Seamus (James Pearse) Finn was born in 1917, Enna (Eithne Agnes) was born in 1918 and Ita Margaret in 1920. There are just a couple of pieces of correspondence remaining from those years. The first one written before Enna was born- the two following are obviously written while May was holiday in Togherstown leaving baby Enna with a nurse at home.

Summer/Autumn 1918 before Eanna was born

Tell me how they got on with the house in Kingstown- or have you any change of opinion on conscription[72] etc. This is a heavenly day here. It looks as if the weather was up I have no news that I can think of. I am keeping grand myself. I hope you are & don't be lonely you will have trouble time enough. After Christmas[73] you will be wishing you made the best of the few quite (sic) hours when you had them. Avoid the flue[74] at any cost I was glad to hear you were praying for us we want them all Bye Bye now best love from the Babby[75] & myself to my own good old hubby

May

192...
Togherstown

Friday[7]

My dearest James,
I was anxiously looking out for late news from you this morning Mondays paper and Wed's were very stale as we have heard of course that they rebelled but we have heard so many other reports such as 200 men men more arrested another strike etc. That I don't know what to do so I have almost entirely to wait over here till Monday or Tuesday I would have gone on Sat. If I had heard to today   I

This picture shows May about 1919 with Shea and Enna

was very relieved to get your telegram it was thoughtful of you to have sent it I hope all are still keeping well & haven't forgot us altogether Shea I think forgets he has any Dublin relations at all he is as happy as a lord. Going around in the muck, don't mention the muck please, it's awful, he looses (sic) his shoes in it sometimes, he is in bed as I write resting before he goes for a drive on the "white horse" as he says himself. White horse run along the road with Shea, he knows everyone around- I don't know will he won't come home at all

I have nothing particular to tell but I wish I knew how things stand I don't want to go home & be turned back at Mullingar or worse Clonsilla. How lucky I should be away at such a time

Best love to poor Ag[78] and your poor self from Shea & May

Saturday (date unknown)

My dearest James

Imagine my being a week here and never to have written a line to you yet but I was twice as anxious as if I had been writing, I enclose letter I had written to you yesterday you will see I did not know in the least how things stood

1921? Shea and Enna in Togherstown?

And it's too late to go home today, that means I can't go tomorrow or until Tuesday on account of the races in Mullingar[79]. We were over in Moran's yesterday eve and Shea did enjoy the drive, he takes endless interest in everything around the place, he'll be very lonely when he goes home tho' for the first time today he admitted he'd like to home to Daddie, Ag & Katie, he never says a word about Maggie except that she's not to laugh at Shea.

I hope you were not starved while the strike was on I'm glad to hear you are all well I hope Katie continues to mind poor Ag I'm dying to see her and my patient old man

Expect me on Tuesday that 10 train from here

We are enjoying the country today the sun is roasting. If it weren't for that I'd go in the evening train.

Best love to all
May
X Shea's Kiss
Excuse pen etc etc if you like

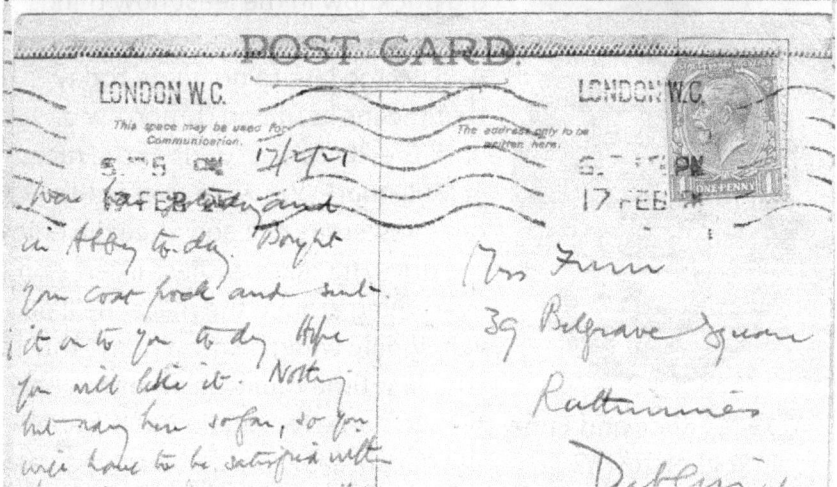

Postcard from London 17 Feb 21 – Picture of Tower of London
Were here yesterday and in Abbey today. Bought you coat frock and sent it on to you today. Hope you will like it. Nothing but navy here so far so you will have to be satisfied with the colour.
Had your letter also note from Shé. Love

Postscript to the letters

The years 1916 to 1918 were full of changes and rumours of changes for everyone in Ireland. The war of Independence gathered strength from the harsh treatment of the insurgents and non-combatants. A war of attrition was carried on. From the British government's point of view some form of home rule was all that was on the bargaining table.

At the end of 1921 and coming into the beginning of 1922, there were intense discussions about the timing and the form of transfer of power from the Castle Administration to the new Free State (Saorstád Éireann) government. The Castle Administration was perceived as being tainted with nepotism, inefficiency and arrogance. Some supported the idea of bringing in all new 'politically correct' men at least at the top. But the functionality would have to be maintained and once the Civi War began, maintenance became more important. The Castle believed the transition would be very slow and gradual but the other side wanted decisiveness. In this period there were high level meetings to discuss this. Finally a list of 46 "reliable and efficient" civil servants representing all of the departments who the Provisional Government could consult with confidence on the work of the departments was created. I believe JE Finn was on that list though I have not been able yet to confirm it. In later years May would remember how even as James' health failed, he was under pressure to attend meetings and that someone suggested he could be stretchered into the office for a meeting, which she refused.

On the 6th May 1922, with May 7 months pregnant with their 4th child(my father) James Finn died. The Death Cert says "Chronic endocarditis 2.5 years, collapse 5 days". Cousin Jim Finn was pres-

Superintendent Registrar's District _Dublin_						Registrar's District _Rathmines No. 1_				
19.22 .	DEATHS Registered in the District of _Rathmines No. 1_ in the Union of _Dublin_ in the County of _Dublin_									
No. (1).	Date and Place of Death. (2).	Name and Surname. (3).	Sex (4).	Condition. (5).	Age last Birthday (6).	Rank, Profession, or Occupation. (7).	Certified Cause of Death and Duration of Illness. (8).	Signature, Qualification, and Residence of Informant. (9).	When Registered (10).	Signature of Registrar. (11).
447	19.22 Sixth May 39 Belgrave Square	James Finn	M	Married	43	Civil Servant	Chronic endocarditis 2½ yrs. collapse 5 days Certified	J. P. Finn present at death Ben Lui Mount Tallant Avenue	Eleventh May 19.22	P.J. Thomas Registrar.

ent at the death.

In 1919, then, James Finn had caught the flu in the great and terrible flu epidemic of 1918-1919. He survived it (maybe partly because he was already a little older than the typical victim) but he suffered the very commonly seen side-effect of endocarditis, inflammation of the inside lining of the heart chambers and heart valves (endocardium) it leads to general weakness and increased likelihood of stroke and heart attack.

It appears he was sick for some weeks or months before his death. Possibly he had had a massive heart attack on the 1st May 1922 which left them with the likely scenario that he would have another fatal attack. So they tried to prepare.

His will is written in May's handwriting- in all likelihood he did not have the strength to write. Because he was not sure if she would have easy access to his he wrote his last few cheques out to pay the rent on their house and the rest (£84, 1 shilling and 2 pence) in her name, scribbling in the side "May, with dearest Love"

In the event, she did not need to use the check and treasured it, along with all her other memorabilia.

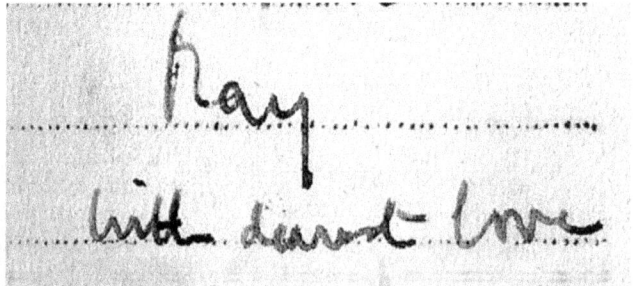

[Main text written in May Finn's handwriting]
This is the last will & testament of Mr. James E Finn of 39 Belgrave Sq Rathmines in the County of Dublin
I appoint my wife May Finn executor hereof. I direct her to pay a sum of £20 to my dear mother Bridget A Finn
The rest residue and remainder of my property of every kind whatsoever including the amount payable on my death under the Civil Service Superannuation Acts I bequeath to my said wife absolutely to be applied by her in her absolute discretion for the benefit of herself and her children
In witness whereof I have hereto set my hand this 2nd of May 1922
Signed by the said Testator as and for his last Will in presence of us present. At the Same time who in his presence and in the presence of each other have hereonto subscribed our names as witnesses.
Illegible solicitors, 3 St Andrew's Street
Nora Finn, Glengyle, Dunville Avenue, Rathmines

Aftermath

May Fay Finn was a survivor; despite her heartbreak she managed. Family stories relate how she took in lodgers, and later went to courses to become qualified in a number of roles which were available to her, chiropody, midwifery, health visitor. Ita Finn relates memories of them selling off the beautiful furniture that James Finn had bought and how a housemaid dramatically left them, saying they were no longer

Photograph from about 1924. Left to right bottom; May, Ita, Enna, Joe, Shea and Nano

the respectable kind of people she had always worked for.
In time she persuaded an adoring bank manager lodger of hers to let her take out a mortgage on a house in the neighbourhood that had come up for sale (very unusual for a woman on her own) and then she set it into flats. In time she had more. She had a gift for it, though she said she was never lucky when she was in the black.

About 1929? Left to right; Shea, May, Enna and Ita

1930s Belgrave Square, Ita's wedding; Front row of adults, Shea, Unknown, Ger Quilligan (groom), Ita, Enna, Joe. May is behind the groom to his right.

Granny May revelled in her many grandchildren and was a strong-willed and (mostly) charming influence on us all encouraging song and creativity. When she suddenly died on St Stephen's Day in 1972 aged 76 there was an aching gap in the centre of our family. But we were comforted to know that she had enjoyed her life to the end. And after she died we found this box of letters, lovingly bound in ribbons, kept after 50 years of widowhood.

I wrote this poem as a teenager a few years after May died

The Grianán

There were flowers in the grass
when my grandmother drank tea
in mismatched china, with the gewgaws
and the little cacti, between billowed net curtains,
showed just moss
under the pear tree
The stone stairs climbed to mysterious places
above, where mustiness pervaded biscuit tins
shrouded by silk
and old extravagant clothes
flannel underwear and useless things
and brown photographs of young girls and lovers
commingling in bedside drawers
A reminiscent sun was shimmering beams
through the all-seeing window
on the chamber of a lady
but the mirror returned
the image of a girl

Notes

1. Mary Seery, wife of James' Thomas, with whom he stayed when in Togherstown
2. May's sister, married the year before, possibly in her first pregnancy
3. Christopher Fay, May's brother and Tommy Seery, James' first cousin.
4. Postman Paddy Lonican
5. James' sister
6. May's cousin, Mary Josephine Wynne
7. Jack Corbett, Jenny's husband was a chemist
8. Possibly Josephine Cunningham, James' relative
9. Unidentified, probably a relative of the Morans, James' cousins. The name is hard to read.
10. All Cunninghams cousins of James?
11. Possibly Jerome Cunningham, James' first cousin.
12. John Cunningham and Ned Fay, May's brother
13. Where the Kiernans lived
14. This reference is unclear to me. The Kilbeggan bride is presumably Gertie Kelly, May's first cousin, who married John Duffy. The Fays seem to have found them "stuck-up"
15. Jack Nolan a neighbour in Togherstown " quite mad at times"
16. Married 2nd February at the church of the Catholic University, Fr Patrick Ivers CC presiding, John Duffy 29 of Rathdrishogue, Castletown
17. John Duffy, married Gertie Kelly
18. Lawrence and Tim, May's brothers
19. Unidentified
20. John Cunningham, James' first cousin.
21. Railway Junction en route to Mitchelstown
22. Mrs Mary Lonican, Postman's wife, Lalstown
23. A cousin of May's- always considered stuck-up
24. Josephine Cunningham
25. Play by Lady Gregory they obviously went to while she

visited

26. Mrs Mary Lonican, Postman's wife, Lalstown
27. Jim Finn, James's cousin
28. Balrath family
29. Seerys' home where James stayed when visiting May.
30. The Kellys had a shop in Castletown
31. Kilbeggan Kellys?
32. Lawrence "Laddie" Fay
33. John Cunningham, James' first cousin.
34. John Cunningham, James' first cousin.
35. Daniel Patrick Gallagher, James' boss, appointed accountant of the NHIC in 1910
36. No relation to James- Joe Finn was a labourer on the Fay farm
37. Kilbeggan Kellys
38. There was controversy about the increased employment of women in the civil service.
39. unknown
40. Mrs Seery's other son
41. A relative of May's from Joanstown
42. May's brothers were no "early birds"; only two of the four married, Gerald at 30 and Tim at 49!
43. Mathew Keenan, 39, blacksmith lived in Ballymorin the next townland to Lockardstown
44. A mhic = my son
45. Reference unclear
46. Thank God
47. Broadstone railway station for Mullingar
48. Hopkins and Hopkins were well-known Dublin jewellers, commissioned to make the original Sam Maguire Cup.
49. Jim Fay would have been her second cousin on the Dardis side.
50. Daniel Patrick Gallagher
51. Jane "Baby" Finn, James first cousin
52. Margaret Moran, James first cousin, daughter of uncle Frank and sister of Fr Frank
53. Keelans Drapers in Mullingar
54. Zeppelin raids were reported on April 3rd

55.   Ellen "Nell" Shiels née Moran, James cousin
56.   Louis Cunningham got engaged
57.   Lissavra Beg where the Morans lived
58.   James' cousin Patrick Moran
59.   Mrs Duffy's wife's brother?
60.   Stanislas Cunningham, James' cousin.
61.   It was on the 29th that they surrendered
62.   There was a great deal of suspicion of civil servants, some
        of it justified since the civil servants formed the backbone
        of the Gaelic League (as I would presume from his com-
        ments James was) and many of those had become radi-
        calised and joined other bodies.
63.   Not a relation, I think
64.   Waistcoat
65.   "Hopkin's has disappeared off the map" Among the build-
        ings destroyed in the fight for Sackville Street during the
        Easter Rising, was Hopkin's and Hopkin's premises."Rifle
        shots had begun to strike the house on the further side
        of the street, a jewellers' shop called Hopkins & Hopkins.
        The impact of these balls on the bricks was louder than
        the sound of the shot which immediately succeeded, and
        each bullet that struck brought down a shower of fine red
        dust from the walls. Perhaps thirty or forty shots in all
        were fired at Hopkins', and then, except for an odd crack,
        firing ceased." James Stephens The Insurrection in Dublin
66.   Of Ballinalack, Westmeath
67.   unidentified
68.   Jocie's sister-in-law
69.   Hopkins announced in the paper that Messrs G Butler &
        Sons in Monument House were offering them a tempo-
        rary place
70.   Daylight saving time was introduced for the first time
        in the British Isles this year and seems to have created
        a great deal of confusion, with people continuing to use
        "old time" alongside "new time"
71.   Eamon Bulfin, born in Argentina was at the GPO and
        raised the Irish flag above the building. Condemned to
        death, because of foreign nationality he was deported to

Argentina after deportation to Frongoch. He returned to
Ireland in 1922

72.   In early 1918 the British government made serious moves
to impose conscription on Ireland and proposed to com-
bine this with limited Home Rule. The reaction from all
camps was very strong and the country was in turmoil for
some time.

73.   Eanna born Christmas

74.   The flu was the eventual cause of his death

75.   Seamus Finn

76.   Railway Junction en route to Mullingar

77.   This is likely to be Spring 1920, major strikes were happening then.

78.   I believe this is a pet name for Enna (Eithne Agnes) She
must have been left in Dublin in the care of a nurse

79.   The Mullingar races were that weekend

I gratefully acknowledge use of images from the Digital Photograph collection of the National Library of Ireland.

www.ingramcontent.com/pod-product-compliance
Lightning Source LLC
Chambersburg PA
CBHW052012090426
42741CB00008B/1658

* 9 7 8 1 9 0 6 8 3 4 2 9 6 *